Buying & Running a
Small Hotel

Practical books that inspire

Mastering Book-Keeping
A complete step-by-step guide to the principles of accounting

Starting your own Business
How to plan and create a successful enterprise

Book-keeping and Accounting for the Small Business
How to keep the books and build financial control over your business

100 Ways to Make Your Business a Sucess

Save Thousands Buying Your Home
A step-by-step guide to reducing the price of a house and the cost of your mortgauge

Please send for a free copy of the latest catalogue to:
How To Books
3 Newtec Place, Magdalen Road,
Oxford OX4 1RE, United Kingdom
email: info@howtobooks.co.uk
www.howtobooks.co.uk

Buying and Running a
Small Hotel

*The complete guide to setting up
and managing your own hotel,
guest house or B & B*

KEN PARKER
3rd edition

howtobooks

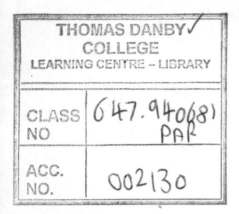

Published by How To Books Ltd, 3 Newtec Place,
Magdalen Road, Oxford OX4 1RE, United Kingdom
Tel: (01865) 793806   Fax: (01865) 248780
email: info@howtobooks.co.uk
www.howtobooks.co.uk

Third edition 2000
Reprinted 2002
Reprinted 2003

British Library Cataloguing in Publication Data
A catalogue record for this book is available from
the British Library

Produced for How To Books by Deer Park Productions
Cover Design by Baseline Arts, Oxford
Typeset by Anneset, Weston-super-Mare,
Printed and bound by Cromwell Press, Trowbridge, Wiltshire

NOTE: The material contained in this book is set out in good
faith for general guidance and no liability can be accepted
for loss or expense incurred as a result of relying in particular
circumstances on statements made in the book. The laws and
regulations are complex and liable to change, and readers should
check the current position with the relevant authorities before
making personal arrangements.

Contents

List of Illustrations

Preface
to the Third Edition

Running a small hotel or guest house is often seen as a glamorous occupation. From the outside, there seem to be so many advantages: being your own boss; not having to commute to work; enjoying an attractive lifestyle; living in an idyllic location. In fact, money for old rope.

Of course there are advantages, but, as with most things in life, there is more to running a hotel than meets the eye.

It is mainly for those who are seriously thinking of entering the business that I have written this book. However, since it deals with the subject comprehensively and includes the most recent legislation, it should also prove extremely valuable to those who are already hoteliers.

Because, almost uniquely, it is so important from everyone's point of view that prospective hoteliers fully understand what is involved before committing themselves, I have devoted the whole of the first chapter to this aspect.

Then, drawing on personal experience, I will guide you through the complexities of becoming a hotelier, how to go about looking for a suitable property, financing and equipping it, and deciding what may be the best way for you to run it.

Since some of you may have decided to take advantage of a depressed market to buy a hotel at a bargain price, my tenth and last chapter addresses the subject of how to survive in a recession.

In addition, there are lists of the legislation affecting the industry and of some trade magazines, a brief explanation of terms used in the trade, a list of further reading and many useful addresses and telephone numbers. Please be aware that regulations do change and organisations often change their names along with contact numbers. As with all business ventures, professional advice should always be sought.

To make description easier, I have used 'hotel' to encompass all like establishments, including guest houses and those offering only bed and breakfast, and have intentionally used the indefinite article 'a' as opposed to the purist's 'an'.

I would like to thank Barclays Bank, Bournemouth and Poole Councils, Bournemouth and Poole College of Further Education, Dorset Business Link, Dorset Fire and Rescue Service, the English and Southern Tourist Boards, ACAS, the Contributions Agency, the

Department of Employment, HM Customs and Excise, the Health & Safety Executive, Ian Perry of South Devon Courts, the Hotel and Catering Training Company, Bournemouth Hotels and Restaurants Association, the British Hospitality Association, Carford Catering Equipment Ltd, Wessex Water, Muriel Paice, Steve de Roeck, John Wain FCA ATII, Mike Wynne-Powell, Milbourne Insurance Services and Commercial Union Assurance Co, for providing me with much useful information.

Ken Parker

1

Deciding Whether Hotel-Keeping is for You

This has to be the most important issue to be addressed, long before you start sending for particulars from agents and scouring newspapers and *Daltons Weekly*. In fact there are many questions to ask before you get to that stage so that you don't waste everyone's time and money, including your own.

Start by asking yourself why you want to be a hotelier.

- Is it because you're fed up with your job and want a change of lifestyle?

- Do you have an overwhelming desire to be your own boss?

- Are you merely looking for something to keep you occupied in your retirement?

- Do you think it's a chance to ease up in some idyllic spot?

- Or have you seen how it's done while you've been on holiday and think you'd like to have a go?

Be very clear on this point — none of the above reasons is good enough on its own. **Being a hotelier is extremely hard work**. And even if you apply yourself 100 per cent, the volume of trade necessary to ensure your business survival may, until you get established, depend to a large extent on such imponderables as the weather and the economic climate. You may need to offer something different — more of that later. For now, there are many other factors that need to be taken into account.

PERSONAL MATTERS

Relationships
In most cases, there will be two or more of you thinking of embarking

on the new venture together and you will hopefully already have fully discussed the subject with your partner and/or family.

Your partner

It is now that you ought to examine how well you get on with your partner (*ie* the person you live with). In running a small establishment you are under each other's feet most of the day, day in, day out. Although you will each have your various jobs to do, there is a lot of overlap and if one of you is snowed under then helping the other out is the name of the game. How well do you get on now when you are both at home and are doing the decorating together or other jobs around the house?

Many relationships thrive on one or both partners being out at work during the day. If yours is one of those, being together all the time might be like lighting the blue touch-paper — except that, once committed, it's not very easy to retire without getting burnt. A lot of couples, including those recently retired, find they need time apart to avoid friction. But whatever you do, don't compare hotel-keeping with retirement — it's anything but!

Once in the hotel business, it is normal to get to know others in the same line. It's surprising how many have to leave their new occupation prematurely to save their marriages. No apologies are offered for labouring this point since it is of the utmost importance.

Your children

If you have children, how would they view a move away from their friends? And is moving schools right for them at their particular stage of education? Kids are surprisingly resilient, but for family harmony you wouldn't want them to hate every moment in their new environment with 'nothing to do' because, for instance, there is no sports centre nearby.

How easily will they be able to find employment in the area you move to? Even if your children have grown up and live away from home, does everyone realise that the times they can visit you, or you them, are very restricted?

Relatives and friends

Maybe you have an elderly relative you visit regularly or keep an eye on. Are you going to be happy moving away? Once you've moved, it is far from easy to leave a hotel full of guests if that relative should become very ill.

Finally, how important is it for you to have friends of long standing nearby, to have bridge or dinner parties on a regular basis, or just to be able to drop round for a chat or a cup of tea? The same guidelines apply to friends visiting as apply to your family. But watch out if you are heading for the coast. You may have heard the phrase, 'once you've moved anywhere near the sea, you find you've got more friends than you knew you had!' It's very true.

Health

You both need to be fit and healthy, even if you do have help, (more of this later) because hotel work is very demanding physically. For example, being on your feet probably more than ever before means that ankles tend to swell up.

You can't feel sorry for yourself when there are guests to be seen to though. They are paying and your problems must never become theirs. You can't afford to be ill and however bad you feel, unless you are totally incapacitated, the show must go on. In dire emergency many guests will rally round to help, but if you're unfortunate enough to be other than in robust good health, think again! And even if you're as strong as an ox, it makes sound sense to have private medical insurance so that you are able to choose the time if you should need to go into hospital.

Temperament

Dealing successfully with members of the public demands skill. They need to be tactfully controlled when they're under your roof so that they don't make your life and those of your other guests a misery. Yet if you marshal them like troops and give them the impression they are there to suit your convenience, they will not return. Although you will be pleased not to see a few of them again, the opposite is the case with the majority — and they are your best source of advertising. So you need to look after them, even pamper them, and not upset them unnecessarily.

You will probably have seen John Cleese in his portrayal of Basil Fawlty. He went on to make a series of training films, exploiting the principle that the best way to teach someone a skill is to show how *not* to do it. (You will learn far more about good hotel-keeping by observing those who do it wrong than the other way round!) Basil simply couldn't bring himself to comply with guests' reasonable requests, let alone the unreasonable ones.

But *you* must. Irrespective of your background, you must be able, putting it bluntly, to take orders. Assuming you go on to owning a hotel, you will find the vast majority of guests give you no problems. But some will, and that's a fact. If you are waiting on tables, not everyone will say 'please' and 'thank you' but will follow what seems to be the British tradition of ignoring waiters as if they were an inferior form of animal life. The fact that you own the place is immaterial!

Could you cope with that? Or, for that matter, could you become a waiter at all? If you've been the boss at work, how will being in a subservient position go down with you?

Not that being a waiter is the beginning and end of your being a servant. How does humping guests' luggage appeal to you? Would you find it beneath your dignity to carry cases for them? It might be more embarrassing if you didn't offer. Not everyone wants their cases carried but they at least like the offer to be made. If you don't treat them as they would like to be treated, do you think they will return? Not on your life! And do you think they will tell their fellow guests? You bet!

As a hotelier, guests are your means of earning a living and therefore need to be treated as you yourself would like to be. It takes a lot of time and effort to build up a good reputation — and about five seconds to destroy it. If you can't bring yourself to pamper your guests, don't become a hotelier.

WHAT TASKS WILL BE INVOLVED?

If you work in an office you may think you are already expected to do far more jobs than the one you were taken on for. As a hotelier, the list of jobs you may have to perform at one stage or another is almost endless. A selection, far from exhaustive, follows. How well do you rate yourself against each?

Cook. . . . .

Waiter. . . . .

Porter . . . .

Tea-maker. . . . .

Washer-up. . . . .

Cleaner . . . .

Gardener. . . . .

Painter . . . .

Decorator . . . .

Chauffeur . . . .

Barman . . . .

Receptionist . . . .

Book-keeper . . . .

Telephonist . . . .

Lackey . . . .

WHO DOES WHAT?

Have you worked out who would do the cooking if you own a hotel? Preparing meals for paying guests is a world apart from cooking for a family, even a large one, and chefs, who do get ill from time to time, can be *very* expensive. In the smaller establishment it is doubtful if you could make a profit if you had to pay a lot of wages, particularly before you get established. So which of you is it to be?

You may have spent a long time in a job you found to be a chore, so it is important that you are able to enjoy *all* the tasks connected with running a hotel, even the washing up. The amount you will get from just a dozen guests will leave you speechless!

And what about the cleaning, bearing in mind that if good food is the most important feature of a hotel, cleanliness comes a close second? And who is going to do the bed-making? Many guests don't like duvets (nor do they like nylon sheets) so bed-making can take up a fair amount of time.

You may not like painting or gardening, but the presentation of your establishment from the outside, including of course the garden, is of prime importance. A scruffy exterior makes people think it is the same on the inside. Doing the lawn can be a bind when you have so little spare time, more so when you get taken for the gardener!

Assuming you decide to run a bar, the barman in a small hotel doesn't just serve drinks and chat to people. He will have to do the setting up, ordering, stocking, glass-washing, cleaning the beer pipes, *etc.* Then there are the accounts, the preparation of menus, tariffs, advertisements, and so on, dealing with the enormous amount of correspondence a hotel generates, sending off brochures, ordering supplies and fetching those which can't be delivered. That's quite apart from maintenance and decoration — and, on a pleasanter note, the banking of your hard-earned receipts.

All these tasks will be discussed in more detail later, but it's as well to know at this early stage so you have some idea who may have to do what. Unfortunately it's not just a case of strutting about in one's finery and taking the money as guests leave!

YOUR INTERIM ASSESSMENT

So that the number of surprises you may get in the future are reduced a little further, try answering the following questions. And before you say, 'People wouldn't do that sort of thing,' they *did*!

1. It is peak season and you have just one room vacant. At 4pm a man telephones from a public call box requiring accommodation for the night, but states he will not arrive until 9pm. Do you:
    (a) Tell him you're not prepared to take the chance he'll turn up?
    (b) Accept the booking, making a note of his name, and keep your fingers crossed? or
    (c) Accept the booking but ask for his name, address, vehicle registration number and/or credit card number?

2. Being a small establishment, you serve a set menu. A guest arrives and, stating she is a vegan, requires a special diet. Do you:
    (a) Tell her she is being most inconsiderate to impose her eating habits on someone else?
    (b) State, if she agrees, you will do what you can within the scope of your resources? or
    (c) Say nothing and buy in food to cater for her needs?

3. In order to have time to wash and change before you open the bar prior to serving dinner, you offer no service between 5.30pm and 6pm. During this time, in spite of having tea-making facilities in the bedroom, a guest wants to be served a tray of tea. Do you:
    (a) Serve the tray of tea with a smile?
    (b) Pretend you don't hear him knocking? or
    (c) Point out the circumstances but still serve him tea?

4. In spite of previously asking a guest not to take your expensive bath towels to the beach, when cleaning the room you notice his towel is missing again. Do you:
    (a) Say nothing but omit to leave a clean one?
    (b) On his return tell him if he does it again you'll put the towel on his bill? or
    (c) Ignore it?

5. At dinner you have served the glass of wine a guest asked for but he

alleges in a loud voice in front of others you have made a mistake. Do you:
- (a) Assert you are correct and tell him he will be charged for it?
- (b) Apologise and serve him a fresh glass of wine? or
- (c) Take it away and bring the same wine back in a clean glass?

6. Smoking is prohibited in your small dining room. A guest insists on lighting up in spite of having been asked politely not to. Do you:
- (a) Ignore it to save embarrassment to other guests?
- (b) See him afterwards privately and require him to leave if he can't stick to the rules? or
- (c) Forcefully extinguish his cigarette and escort him out of the hotel?

7. When cleaning the room, you notice a guest has cracked the wash-hand basin and has gone out without telling you.
On his return do you:
- (a) Say nothing, having ordered a replacement?
- (b) Tell him his shortcomings and put the cost of the replacement on his bill? or
- (c) Point out to him the importance of notifying damage, however caused, and get it repaired as soon as possible?

8. You have the hotel telephone by your private quarters door just off the dining room. In spite of there being a payphone available for guests' use, you find one using your own telephone to make a private call. Do you:
- (a) Cut him off by depressing the cradle?
- (b) Time the call, point out when he's finished the error of his ways and charge him accordingly? or
- (c) Pretend you haven't noticed?

9. A guest approaches you and apologises profusely for having just damaged your prize cheese-plant. You go with him to see and he tells you he was just having you on. Do you:
- (a) Tell him to grow up?
- (b) Smile and pretend to share the joke?
- (c) Humour him, pretend there is damage and say the cost of a replacement will go on his bill?

10. About to leave, a guest in settling up asks for two bills, one for the exact amount and one enhanced to present to his firm for

reimbursement. Do you:
(a) Politely decline his request and give him just the correct bill?
(b) Ask him for his firm's telephone number so that you can tell the managing director of his fiddle? or
(c) Accede to his request so as not to upset him?

Answers

1.(a) 1 point; (b) 2 points; (c) 3 points.
The scourge of hoteliers is the non-appearance of guests who book by telephone at the last minute. Although you may be given false information, by requiring detailed particulars you will probably receive the correct ones and this may persuade a fickle guest to turn up.

2.(a) 1 point; (b) 3 points; (c) 2 points.
Guests should realise that in a small establishment the menu is restricted and that it is unreasonable to expect to be specially catered for without prior notification and acceptance of the situation on both sides.

3.(a) 2 points; (b) 1 point; (c) 3 points.
Some guests will exercise their right to be waited on hand and foot, often just to be awkward or to try you out. If you don't nip it in the bud, your life will be made a misery.

4.(a) 3 points; (b) 1 point; (c) 2 points.
Your charges are unlikely to compensate for having towels lost or stained by oil, *etc.* Having given one warning, another is unlikely to have any effect. By not changing the towel (and later replacing it with an old one) the message may well get home.

5.(a) 1 point; (b) 2 points; (c) 3 points.
If you *know* you're right, the guest has proved he doesn't know what he's drinking. (A not uncommon occurrence!) Replacing only the glass will keep you in pocket and he won't have the nerve to show himself up again!

6.(a) 2 points; (b) 3 points; (c) 1 point.
A no-smoking rule in a small dining room is reasonable for everyone's comfort. The inconsideration of one must not be allowed to spoil the enjoyment of the majority.

7. (a) 2 points; (b) 1 point; (c) 3 points.
There's a good chance your insurance excess will mean the repairs are down to you. However, damage will occur from time to time and the

least a guest can do is tell you.

8. (a) 1 point; (b) 3 points; (c) 2 points.
When you're paying for a separate telephone for guests' use, it's inexcusable that anyone should use your private line. It could lose you bookings.

9.(a) 1 point; (b) 2 points; (c) 3 points.
There's no accounting for some people's sense of humour!

10.(a) 3 points; (b) 1 point; (c) 2 points.
If you are a party to his fiddle and it comes to light, you could find yourself in the dock. The tax inspector would never trust you again — and who could blame him?

Your score
If you scored **23 points** or more, you are a natural and should take up hotel-keeping immediately! You realise you need to be a psychologist to be a successful hotelier and in moments of guest-induced crisis you need to pass the pressure straight back on to the guilty party.

Twelve to 22 points means you may still be successful, but are prepared to accept the customer is always right and that some will derive great pleasure from keeping you on the end of a short piece of string.

Under **12 points** and if *Fawlty Towers* comes back, you should audition for the part originally played by John Cleese! He used to *say* what most hoteliers just *think*.

How did you do? Take heart from the fact that those guests who cause the trouble are very much in the minority — but they are there.

CAN I AFFORD TO BUY A HOTEL?

A number of assumptions have now been made:

- There are no family problems standing in your way.
- Your health is good.
- You are temperamentally suited to hotel work.
- You have a fair idea of what is involved.
- You are prepared to have a go.

To sort out whether or not you have enough money to buy a hotel is the next logical step.

Your initial calculations

If you don't already have a property to sell or substantial capital of your own (meaning that you are looking to borrow the full purchase price), save yourself and others a great deal of time right now — forget it!

The bane of a business agent's life (and estate agents') is the large number of time-wasters that have to be dealt with. Every day people make serious offers on commercial properties when they've not a penny to their name, no property of their own and, therefore, no chance of being a purchaser. One even made it sound an advantage by saying he had nothing to sell and was in consequence a 'cash buyer'. He omitted to say he had no cash!

Selling your own property

Assuming you do not have the cash for your hotel in the bank, your first step as far as money is concerned is to work out how much capital you can raise.

Valuing your property

Your own house or business is a starting point. The present system may be responsible for keeping agents' selling commissions high, but you can get a free valuation on your house by telling them you are thinking of selling and implying they may get your instructions.

If the first agent you approach wants a fee, there are many who won't insist, especially after you have chatted them up. You have already decided you are potentially a good hotelier and you can therefore talk people round to your way of thinking. It won't be long before you are talking people into spending time and money in your hotel, so the estate agent should be a pushover!

Valuations are a very grey area. In the commercial world a reasonably accurate price can be put on a business by applying various factors relating to turnover and profit margins as well as assessing the 'bricks and mortar' value, *ie* what the building itself is worth apart from trading considerations.

Domestic properties are, however, a different kettle of fish. You may find yourself having qualms when a sales negotiator appears looking as if he's just been let out of school, but there are plenty more agents around. You need one who has substantial experience of property prices in your area over several years. Be direct — ask how long he has been in business and where.

The experienced negotiator will take many factors into account when calculating a value, including the size and type of property, the condition, what price similar properties in the area have fetched (not what they've been offered at), the state of the market and, of prime importance, the location.

Location is the most important consideration. All sorts of things can be done to improve a property but there is nothing you can do to improve where it is. It erodes the value (as well as the foundations) if, for example, lorries are continually thundering past your door on their way to the newly-opened Council tip up the road.

We'll be talking about location in detail when we discuss how to search for your ideal hotel but, for the moment, bearing all considerations in mind, you will want to end up knowing an amount you can realistically expect to get on what is probably your most valuable asset.

If your property is over-priced it has very little, if any, chance of selling. So get more than one valuation to make sure the first one is on the right track.

Choosing an agent
Be realistic. The other advantage of getting in more than one agent is so that you can compare their degree of professionalism and judge who might best market your property when the time comes.

Sharpening your skill of being able to weigh people up will come in very useful when you are operating your hotel. Always ask what an agent's commission rates are and express surprise if they exceed what another has quoted.

You should not necessarily always go for the cheapest, but if the service is comparable the difference a quarter of 1 per cent will make on the sale of a £100,000 property, to include VAT, is almost £300. It does well to remember that most agents' fees are negotiable, particularly when competition is fierce.

Working out the figures
In the end, the property you currently own will fetch what someone is prepared to pay for it, no more, no less; the time-honoured estate agents' phrase, 'We have a lot of demand for this type of property,' uttered in an attempt to win your instructions, can be taken with a pinch of salt. Understandably, they adopt the attitude that if it's not on their books, they can't sell it.

Overestimating what you will be left with by the time the mortgage, if any, is settled and everyone like the estate agent, solicitor, removal firm, *etc* has been paid can seriously frustrate your plans.

Other assets
When looking at what else you own, consider selling anything of value

you don't really want, or cannot afford to keep. You ought not to borrow more than you need nor should you leave money earning a low rate in the building society and then pay double in loan interest.

THE FINAL ASSET FIGURE

By the time you have done all your calculations, you will end up with an asset figure which, converted into cash, will help you buy your hotel.

If at this juncture you are absolutely determined to be a hotelier and you are sure you can afford it, then selling your present home, putting your furniture into store and moving into temporary accommodation will have two main advantages:

- You will *know* what you've got to spend;
- Not being in a chain will put you in a strong bargaining position to make your purchase, as well as reducing the risk of missing out on the hotel you really want because you can't find a buyer at the crucial time.

CHECKLIST

Are you:

- In robust good health?
- Sure no personal or family problems stand in your way?
- Able to cope with the physical demands of hotel work?
- Not too proud to take orders?
- Tolerant enough to be able to deal calmly with awkward guests?
- Prepared to carry out any task, no matter how menial?
- Sure you know what to expect?
- Aware of how much you can afford to spend?
- Fully determined to succeed?

2

Choosing the Right Hotel
for You

WHAT SHOULD WE LOOK FOR?

The last thing you need to do before embarking on the search is to decide exactly what it is you are looking for.

Don't be surprised if you end up with something entirely different to what you are now envisaging. Many do. It is mainly for this reason that agents tend to send out details of everything they have within a buyer's price range. 'That looks nice' is often at odds with the sort of property you thought you wanted. So if the agent is going to send you six-bedroomed properties when you had stipulated 'not less than ten', just throw the unwanted details away. After all, you're not paying for them.

Now is the time to open a dossier on your business plans; an inexpensive ring binder will do nicely. You know roughly how much you will have to spend. Now is the time to record what you might be spending it on.

Which location?

Just as location is important in a house, as you will find out when you come to sell, so it is of the utmost importance when you are choosing not only a home, but your main source of income.

Do you already have a location in mind? If it is your favourite holiday haunt, ask yourself why you enjoy it so much. Is it because it's always packed with holidaymakers? Or is it the opposite — peaceful, uncrowded, relaxing?

Your familiar holiday haunt might *not* be a good idea. Remember, you are looking for a business and to succeed businesses must make a profit.

- Few people can mean empty bedspaces.
- Empty bedspaces mean less profit.
- Less profit (or none at all) can spell disaster.

As you will find out when you start looking, there are many types of

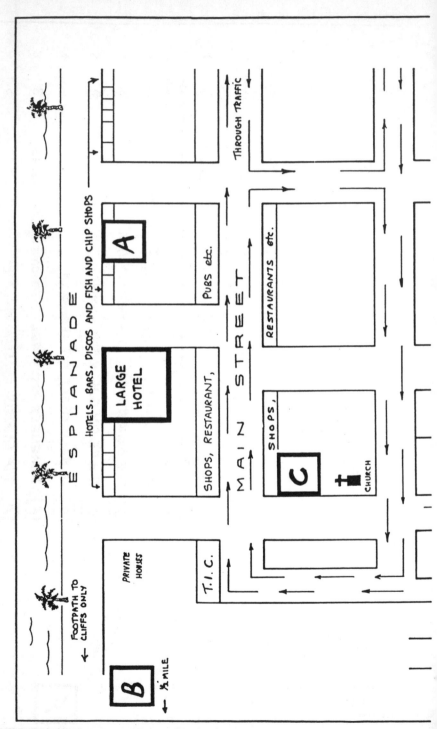

Fig. 1. Plan of Surfbourne.

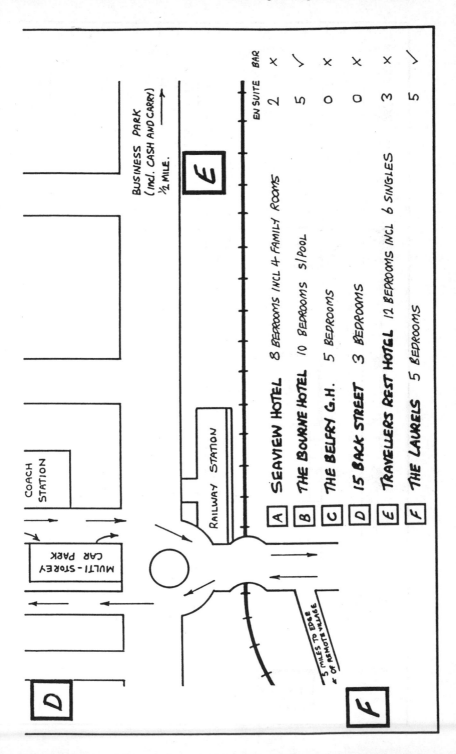

		EN SUITE	BAR
A	SEAVIEW HOTEL 8 BEDROOMS INCL 4 FAMILY ROOMS	2	✗
B	THE BOURNE HOTEL 10 BEDROOMS S/POOL	5	✓
C	THE BELFRY G.H. 5 BEDROOMS	0	✗
D	15 BACK STREET 3 BEDROOMS	0	✗
E	TRAVELLERS REST HOTEL 12 BEDROOMS INCL 6 SINGLES	3	✗
F	THE LAURELS 5 BEDROOMS	5	✓

BUSINESS PARK
(incl. CASH AND CARRY)
½ MILE. →

COACH STATION

MULTI - STOREY CAR PARK

RAILWAY STATION

5 MILES TO EDGE OF REMOTE VILLAGE

location. A few of them are shown on the sketch plan of Surfbourne, a mythical small, but expanding, seaside town with good beaches (see Figure 1).

Are you aware that a number of large retailing companies employ staff specially to sort out locations for their stores? Many factors are taken into account, *eg* proximity to car parks, bus stops and terminals, railway stations and the routes people take from one amenity to another.

If *your* hotel is the sort that relies heavily on passing trade, its location (and its presentation) can be vital.

Not every hotel is in the same price bracket, nor do the same criteria necessarily apply to hotels as to stores; but take each location shown on the sketch plan in turn and list what you consider to be the advantages and disadvantages of each from the point of view of attracting passing trade. Many are obvious, others not so obvious. Which location would you prefer to occupy, and why?

- 'A' is in the prime location for casual trade. When holidaymakers go to the seaside the majority prefer a sea view, at least from the lounge or dining area if not from their bedrooms. The fact that there is plenty of competition around means your hotel will need to stand out. When potential money-spenders are weighing up which door to knock on, a smart, clean appearance can tilt the balance. Yet, to go too far in making your hotel stand out could be unviable since your prices would have to stay roughly in line with those charged by similar hotels. The provision of off-street parking and better facilities could give you an edge.

- 'B' is away from the main stream and may well be overlooked by a large number of holidaymakers. Yet it has the advantages of a sea view and accessibility to the beach. It could appeal to those requiring a quieter holiday — once they know about it. Incidentally, it is highly unlikely that planning permission would be granted for any directional signs.

- 'C' is right in the middle of town but without a sea view and there is a busy main road to be crossed to get to the beach. Most people visiting the town would come across it since they tend to gravitate from the various amenities towards the sea. Providing there isn't a surfeit of available bedspaces, it should fill up regularly from passing trade. Noise could be a problem, particularly if the church has a chiming clock.

- 'D' is situated in a side street, well off the beaten track and hardly in a good position for providing a regular, reliable living. New owners will need a lot of help in getting known. Both 'C' and 'D' may appeal to the business traveller. Parking and off-loading supplies could be serious problems.

- 'E' will derive much of its trade from business customers. However, most visitors arriving at the railway station will not see it. If an advertisement in the railway station were possible, it could greatly enhance trade. Its saving grace might be the business park, where its presence should be well advertised.

- 'F' is in the location least liked by many bank managers who are asked to lend money. In a remote village the amount of passing trade is virtually nil. The rateable value should be lower than for town properties and there will almost certainly be no parking problems. There will just as likely be no streetlights. If you are a townie, do you know what real darkness is? With no moon or starlight, the blackness is nothing short of eerie. Being on your own, how will you get on with the locals? Will tradesmen be willing to deliver supplies without stipulating what to you may appear an unrealistic minimum order? Are you financially equipped to cope with a short season or will you need to diversify until your advertisements bear fruit?

Unless you are in a location where you have a captive audience, *eg* 'A' and 'C,' why, you may ask, do you need to advertise when the present owner has built up a substantial following?

The answer lies in the question; it is the *present* owner who has built up the trade, not you. Many visitors return only to see the proprietors they know. It has been known for an owner's appeal to override daily burnt breakfasts!

For potential clients to ring off when they realise there has been a change of owner is commonplace. As with shares, evidence of past performance is no guarantee for the future!

If you find you have decided on a location, or if you receive details of a hotel you really like the sound of (enlarged on in Chapter 3), a telephone call to the local **Tourist Information Centre** for statistics about visitors to the area, compared with bedspaces available, could prove invaluable.

Returning to the subject of stores, customers are unwittingly channelled into parts of the store where they are likely to make an impulse buy. In towns, particularly where there are peaks of activity such as festivals and conferences, the hotels that do best are those that people come across without really looking and are immediately impressed with.

Try it! It is only by being there and exploring (on foot in the town) that you can accurately assess the level of trade and the potential, a word used by many agents to lure the buyer into thinking a business can do better than it has before.

Some questions to ask
This sort of analysis is also the only way to accurately assess the points we have discussed earlier:

- How much trade is likely to be derived from passers-by?
- What is the level of tourism at various times of the year in regard to available bedspaces?
- If advertising seems necessary, where do most visitors come from?
- How close and accessible are the major amenities?
- What are the views like?
- How much noise is around, *eg* from traffic, trains, dogs, aeroplanes, church clocks, farms, and so on?
- Are there any smells from farmyards, factories, that might upset your guests?
- How easy is parking for you, potential guests who want to stop and enquire, residents and delivery vehicles?
- Do you honestly think a hotel in your chosen location is likely to provide you with a viable living?

How many bedrooms?
Ask yourself:

- How hard do you want to work?
- Do you want to employ staff?
- Do you need a high turnover?

To a large extent, the number of bedrooms you require will depend on your answers.

If there are just two of you and you intend to run your hotel virtually unaided, coping with more than twelve guests might well be beyond your capabilities. If they are all eating at the same time, the equivalent of six double tables will be the most you will be able to serve *efficiently*.

A small increase may be coped with if mealtimes are staggered, but otherwise, for one person to serve twelve guests with three or four courses, perhaps plus wine, will require much alacrity. This is assuming you want to do the job properly. Many people, especially those on holiday, do not mind waiting for their food, but a lot *do* mind and will soon tell you so, if only by not returning.

● A simple rule: if you are going to have more than twelve guests, equating with six double bedrooms, you will need help in the dining room.

As with all businesses, the most expensive commodity is labour and, unless you are very lucky, staff will not do the job exactly, if anything like, the way you would do it yourself.

The more bedrooms you have above six, therefore, the more staff you will need to employ, not only for waiting on tables but for cleaning, washing up, *etc*. Yet you should be aiming to make a profit and, generally speaking, the fewer the bedrooms, the lower your takings.

If there are just two of you and you want to avoid employing staff, ten guests or five double/twin bedrooms in a location where you could have a small bar would be ideal.

Your own accommodation

Before you ink in the number of bedrooms you are aiming for, do consider your own accommodation needs. Most business people who 'live above the shop' compromise on what they would really like.

How far are you prepared to compromise? Would *you* live in a ramshackle old caravan round the back so that paying guests can occupy your bedroom? Would *you* sleep in a tent on the lawn for the same reason? Some do.

Running a hotel is extremely hard work and when you have finished for the day you may feel you need something a lot more comfortable than a sleeping bag.

Try to sort out your own accommodation to be as spacious, comfortable and private from that of the guests as possible. Preferably, have your own en suite bathroom.

WHAT FACILITIES SHOULD BE PROVIDED?

Bathrooms

People have got used to travelling abroad and being provided with an en suite bathroom. It is no wonder that demand in the UK is rising. When you go on holiday, do you insist on an en suite bathroom?

So again, before you finally decide how many bedrooms to go for (assuming en suite bathrooms are not already provided) do consider whether you should allow for converting any into bathrooms.

As the Chairman of Trafalgar House once said about accommodation aboard the QE2, it is easy to let the luxury suites; most difficult are the ordinary cabins. This is often the case with hotel rooms. Your most luxurious rooms will sell most easily, in spite of costing more. Basic rooms are often not so easy. There are exceptions to every rule, and your location and the type of clientele which normally visits the area can turn this on its head.

Just to clear up one point — the difference between en suite and private bathrooms:

- **En suite** means forming a self-contained unit: the guest does not have to step outside the bedroom to go to the bathroom.
- **Private bathrooms**, far less acceptable, might be next door, along the corridor, or worse still, right at the end of the corridor, with the room number on it.

En suite bathrooms are the standard required by a growing number of guests today. And they expect them to be clean, smart and well-decorated. The bathroom is the first place many guests look at. Think seriously about providing en suite bathrooms when calculating how many bedrooms you require.

For the disabled

Disabled people need to take holidays and to be able to stay at hotels in the same way as anyone else. Yet few establishments cater adequately for them. This is due to change. **The Disability Discrimination Act 1995** lays down new rights for the disabled and is designed to prevent discrimination. By 2005 it is anticipated that all service providers will be obliged to provide proper access and facilities for the disabled. Planning for this change well in advance is recommended. For information on how to go about it, see page 205.

Other facilities

It is also worth thinking about whether the sort of establishment you have in mind should provide more luxurious facilities, perhaps an indoor swimming pool, a small gymnasium and/or a sauna.

In the right location, you might be able to convert a ten-bedroomed property into luxury five- or six-bedroomed accommodation, charge accordingly and employ less or even no staff at all.

WHAT SORT OF FOOD SHOULD BE PROVIDED?

This has to be a serious consideration when weighing up what sort of hotel to go for. Guests have expectations according to the type of hotel they are staying at.

As has been said before, it is unlikely that you will be able to afford a chef at first, if at all. In most cases, therefore, the dishes have to be within your own capabilities. Your personality and charm *may* prevail over the fact that you burn everything you put within a metre of an oven, but serving overdone food is *not* recommended. Guests just might see the funny side once or twice, but not on a regular basis.

Breakfast

Since you will not get away with serving Continental breakfast every day, you will at least need to be able to cook a decent English breakfast. Easy? That depends on how involved your breakfast menu is. Would you like a fried egg, bacon and sausage to be dumped (no matter how nicely) in front of you every morning? Take a look at the sort of basic breakfast menu you might prefer.

Breakfast

Fruit juice (orange, grapefruit, pineapple or apple)

***

Cereal (Cornflakes, Shredded Wheat, Weetabix, All Bran)

or

Fruit (grapefruit segments, stewed prunes)

***

Cooked breakfast (fried egg, grilled bacon, grilled sausage, fried bread, fried tomato)

or

Eggs (boiled, poached or scrambled on toast)

or

Fish (haddock or kipper fillet)

***

Brown or white toast
Marmalade and honey '
Tea or coffee

If you think you can work out all the various permutations, just wait until a resourceful houseful of guests get to work! Particularly where children are involved, you may in addition need to find baked beans, or fish fingers, or . . .?

Preparing breakfast from a menu which offers choice is clearly far from simple. Various items of commercial equipment, discussed in Chapter 6, can help but it's still not easy, particularly if guests all sit down at the same time.

Daytime meals

If you think you can cope with preparing breakfast, how do you feel about other meals?

Morning coffees, snack lunches and afternoon teas are quite easy to prepare and serve but are, to say the least, time-consuming. In the absence of a reasonable volume of trade, they would not be worth doing and would not justify the many hours spent on stand-by, let alone the wastage of food.

Providing such meals, especially for non-residents, is a matter of judgement and could be tried as a diversification to boost turnover, discussed in Chapter 9.

Evening meals

However, what might fill most intending hoteliers with foreboding is the provision of evening meals.

The first thing to remember is there is little similarity in providing a dining room full of paying guests with an evening meal and preparing dinner for friends.

Private dinner guests will usually say nothing if they have to wait while you ditch the burnt starter and rustle up an alternative; or if the meat is tough; or if the vegetables have been cooked to death; or if the dessert looks awful because the cream curdled. Paying guests *might* not say anything but at the least will let you know by not returning, or, worse still, by feigning illness and going home early. Even worse, by becoming genuinely ill and suing you!

Before you feel too bad, *every* cook, no matter how experienced, has disasters in the kitchen. The secret is to keep that sort of information from your guests and to avoid regular mishaps.

Since it would be unusual to have Egon Ronay as a guest, you don't have to be able to turn out a gourmet meal — unless you advertise such food. Most guests prefer good, wholesome food which, to coin a well-used phrase, 'hasn't been mucked about'. It must, though, be competently prepared and cooked to a timetable. Can you manage that? Or would it worry you too much?

Going back to our example hotels, the proprietors of all of those in the town centre could probably get away with not doing an evening meal. Providing there are enough restaurants, pubs and the like within easy reach, guests will often accept a B & B situation. But not all will like it. Many like to go out for the day, come back, tidy up and relax for the evening. Often parents with young children, having worn them out, prefer to get them to bed reasonably soon after an evening meal and maybe go out on their own, leaving you to babysit. To have to hunt round with tired youngsters for somewhere to eat might, at the least, be inconvenient. The following year they will look for a hotel that gives them the facility they want.

Any hotel that is in a quieter spot, such as The Laurels and to a lesser extent The Bourne, might find it difficult to resist doing evening meals. In out-of-the-way situations, if there is no good pub or restaurant nearby the provision of dinner is almost a must.

A good cook with flair can enjoy preparing a mixture of plain and not-so-plain fare for dinner guests. It would not, however, be a good idea to offer *cordon bleu* cooking unless the cook has been formally trained or, through much practice, has complete confidence. Advertising *nouvelle cuisine* could be a disaster. The term has come to be seen by many as a euphemism for small portions, vastly overpriced.

Finally, consider the complications of providing a choice of dinner menu, especially an *à la carte* one, and staggering mealtimes (discussed fully in Chapter 9). If you think the sort of establishment you are looking at would be expected to offer this sort of service, make sure you are confident of your capabilities.

SHOULD WE RUN A BAR?

The decision may not be as simple as it seems. In order to be allowed by law to serve alcoholic drinks, you need a licence which is issued by a Magistrates' Court.

Some **Licensing Justices** (as the group of magistrates who hear such applications are called) are loath to grant too many licences. You may need to show that no public nuisance nor threat to public order or public safety is likely to result.

Although there is a right of appeal to the Crown Court, judges normally uphold the policy decisions of the local magistrates. If it's important for you to have a bar where none exists at present, it would

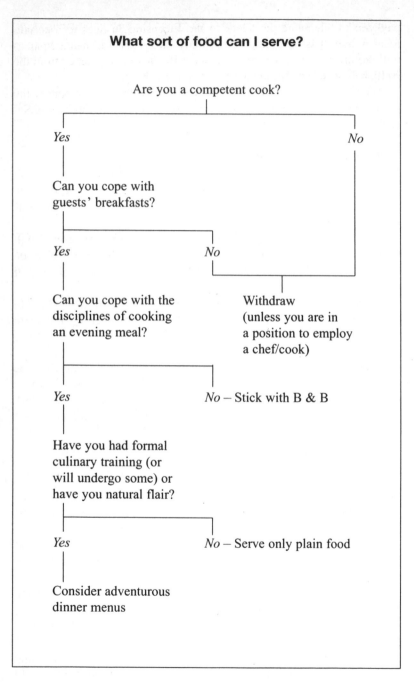

Fig. 2. What sort of food can I serve?

pay you to telephone the Clerk to the Licensing Justices to ascertain local policy. It is becoming increasingly likely that Licensing Justices will require new licensees to obtain a certificate of competence from the **British Institute of Innkeeping**. (See page 178.)

The police make enquiries about every applicant, and can oppose the granting of a licence if they find an intending licensee not to be of good character, particularly in regard to the licensing laws.

The resort hotel without bar

Seaview Hotel could well be an example of this. This sort of hotel may provide an evening meal, probably served early for the benefit of young families. Although it is not obligatory to cater for youngsters, it is normal in this type of location.

Sensible, solid furniture and not too many breakables around will keep the owner's blood pressure from rising too high, especially when the occasional destructive family stays. Unless you are tolerant of children, it would be better not to run a family hotel.

If you provide an evening meal, you might like to offer wine. Should you be unable to obtain a licence and yet still wish to serve wine, there are two compromises you could make:

- Serve alcohol-free/very low alcoholic content wine (it needs to be less than 1.2 per cent alcohol to be termed non-alcoholic).
- Let guests provide their own wine and put up with the extra work involved, like chilling it and providing and washing up glasses.

Staff, perhaps only to help at mealtimes, will be necessary.

The resort hotel with bar

This may well apply to the Bourne Hotel, the owners of which could be the holders of a residential licence. Being away from the hub of activity, it is likely their guests prefer the quieter atmosphere.

Many of them will have responded to advertising, both local and national, and there are no neighbouring hotels to influence the tariff. Consequently, such a hotel could be run as a superior establishment providing a good quality evening meal and a good, if modest, wine list. Providing guests can find someone to serve them, they can drink at any time without being restricted to normal licensing hours (see page 157).

It's nothing short of a disaster when you spend literally hours behind the bar and serve only two halves of shandy all evening, particularly when you have to be up early the next (or the same) morning to start preparing breakfasts. A bar needs firm control and good judgement to make a profit (see Chapter 9).

B and B establishments

Here we are talking about properties such as The Belfry and 15 Back Street.

Bed and breakfast only, using perhaps only one or two rooms, is often offered by those looking for other than a main supporting income. Such people are known in the hotel trade as 'pirates,' and some of the legislation which applies to larger establishments is relaxed for them.

Providing a property is predominantly domestic, as opposed to commercial, and does not cater for more than six resident guests, the owners are exempt from paying business rates. Further, subject to certain exceptions (shown in Chapter 3), and again providing not more than six guests are catered for, it may be unnecessary to comply with fire regulations. Several hundred if not thousands of pounds can be saved if neither of these two provisions apply, but your income will be restricted to what can be earned from a maximum of six guests. Having said that, with only six guests the right premises can provide a good income. Even £15 per person per night for 40 weeks of the year would produce a turnover of £25,000 pa.

In normal circumstances the net profit from providing just bed and breakfast is high, but the disadvantage of a small B and B is the low turnover. It can be ideal for a couple; one running the B and B while the other goes out to work. Obviously the time commitment is much less than if service is offered after breakfast has been cleared away.

The commercial hotel

The aptly named Travellers' Rest falls into this category.

When you set out to accommodate the business traveller, you are aiming at a different type of client to the holidaymaker. Usually an early start is made, meaning that you will almost certainly have to provide breakfasts at different times. There is then a long void until your guests return in the evening.

Most business people travel on their own. It is therefore best to be able to provide single rooms to save tying up doubles with single occupancy. Business travellers need to make out sales figures, reports, *etc* at the end of the day, so thought must be given to providing the right facilities, which would have to include the use of a telephone and maybe a fax.

This hotel will usually have empty beds between when most business travellers go home on Friday and return on Monday. Unless other guests are attracted by special offers, weekend breaks, *etc* the turnover can be seriously reduced. If you can afford to do so, it may suit you to take things easy at weekends.

Depending on nearby facilities for obtaining food in the evenings, you may find you need to provide dinner. Again, flexibility is often called for as meetings can go on longer than anticipated. It might be sensible for the modest hotelier to provide substantial snacks as required.

As far as a bar is concerned, individual circumstances would have to dictate the strategy, bearing in mind the proximity to other drinking houses.

The charges of a small commercial hotel are likely to be well within the business person's allowance, so can prove popular with all but the top brass. Such a hotel is worth considering for a relatively limited time commitment.

The country hotel

Bearing in mind what has been said about the possible attitude of lenders, a property such as The Laurels can be a rewarding venture, even if every day turns out to be long and demanding.

Business guests will be few and far between. Most of the clientele will be seasonal holidaymakers looking for a restful break in a peaceful, relaxed atmosphere. For a flourishing trade it will almost certainly be necessary to provide evening meals, and the ability to serve alcoholic drinks could be beneficial for all concerned.

Depending on circumstances, you may decide it is better to operate on a limited season, *eg* Easter to the end of October, perhaps reopening for the highly lucrative Christmas and New Year period.

Assuming you are able to provide a high standard of food, you could decide to offer restaurant meals to non-residents or even, providing you have the necessary room and facilities, to run a bar for non-residents as well as your residents. But beware! Once your residents decide the service they are getting is inferior because of the presence of non-residents, or they have nowhere to put their car in the car park because of visitors' vehicles, you will lose their custom.

On the staff front, depending on how hard you are prepared to push yourself, you may not need any extra help. On the other hand, someone to make beds and clean the bedrooms, perhaps to help wait on tables, do the laundry or help in the garden, would reduce your workload considerably.

In such a property you will have the opportunity to stamp your personality on the hotel and provide something different. For example, you might offer a superb standard of food, speciality weekends, guided country walks, you name it.

A country hotel is worth considering if you want to avoid the 'bucket and spade brigade'.

WHAT TYPE OF OWNERSHIP?

Sole proprietorship

As implied, this is where the owner trades alone, whether it is in the owner's name or that of the hotel.

The sole proprietor stands or falls by the decisions made, is answerable to no one (except as required by law), takes all the profits, but is personally liable for all the debts. All personal possessions are at risk in the event of debt enforcement.

Partnerships

Unless it is necessary to pool resources, be they for finance or expertise, it will rarely be a good idea to consider a partnership.

Up to 20 persons can form a partnership and, generally speaking, each shares the profits and debts of the business.

In the case of a husband and wife, few legal problems are likely to ensue, even if the partnership breaks up, since both are considered in law to be equally liable. However, as with all partnerships, if one or more partners disappear, the other(s) may have to settle any debts that might arise.

In the case of a partnership with other relatives or with friends, the situation is fraught with danger. Although it is not strictly necessary to have a partnership drawn up legally, with anything other than a husband and wife situation it is absolutely essential. (Some say highly advisable with husbands and wives.) Have you noticed how easy it is for different couples who go on holiday together to fall out? And that is over a very short period. And how many times have you heard of a wife running off with her husband's best friend, or vice versa? Food for thought if two couples are thinking of going into partnership together.

In a purely business situation, a frequent source of disagreement is over who puts in the most (or the least) effort. 'He does the grafting while I do the thinking' is not an attitude easily accepted by a hard-working partner.

If because of the need to pool resources you decide a partnership is for you, discuss the matter fully with each and every potential partner and draw up a list of points which could lead to controversy. They include:

- How much capital will be introduced by each.

- What obligations there are, if any, to introduce further capital.
- How profits and losses are to be shared out and dealt with.
- How much each is to take in remuneration.
- The responsibilities of each partner as regards duties and management.
- Who will make major decisions and what happens if agreement cannot be arrived at.
- Whether any partner should have limited liability (see below).
- What arrangements will be made for holidays.
- What happens in the case of death or illness.
- Under what terms and conditions the partnership can be dissolved.
- How shares are to be valued in the event of the departure of a partner.
- The rights of each partner to sell or assign shares.

If agreement on the above points cannot be readily agreed in a hypothetical situation, what chance does a partnership stand when it is for real?

Once all matters have been resolved, the list should be handed to a solicitor experienced in such contracts for it to be formally drawn up.

Limited partnerships

This usually occurs when someone is putting up money but has no interest or say in how the business is run. (Sometimes referred to as a sleeping partner.) By law, details of such cash injections have to be notified to the **Registrar of Companies**.

Should the business fail, the limited partner's liability is restricted to the amount of capital introduced. All such liabilities, rights to profits, *etc*, should be included in the contract by an experienced solicitor.

Private limited company

Virtually anyone can set up a limited company. Two directors, one of whom may be the company secretary, are required and for fees totalling a few hundred pounds a company can be bought 'off the shelf'.

The advantages are:

- The kudos of calling yourself a managing director.
- The shareholders' liability is limited in the event of bankruptcy (though banks and other lenders may negate this by requiring personal guarantees).

The disadvantages are:

● Increased administration, including shareholders' meetings.
● Increased paperwork, including having to have the accounts audited.
● Increased taxation and National Insurance contributions.

It will rarely be an advantage to run a small hotel as a limited company. An experienced solicitor will advise on this subject.

CHECKLIST

Do you know. . .

● The various types of hotel available?
● What sort of hotel you want?
● What size of hotel you want?
● How to check out an area?
● What standard of food you can provide?
● The facilities you want to aim for?
● How the various types of ownership affect you?
● Whether you have the confidence to proceed?

3

Making the Search

STARTING FROM SCRATCH

What legislation will we have to comply with?

Although the list of Acts of Parliament relating to hotels is far from short, it need not be daunting. They have been drawn up to protect guests, the people who will provide you with a living. You will therefore need a working knowledge of what you must comply with, not only when you have started to run a hotel but when you are considering which to go for.

If, for example, **Fire Regulations** have not been complied with, the cost of implementing them could be considerable and might be high enough to thwart your plans. We shall look at the most important legislation you need to know about before you begin the search in earnest.

Fire regulations

To reduce the likelihood of fire breaking out and in the event of fire to increase the chances of survival, the **Fire Prevention Act 1971** was devised.

It stipulates that where sleeping accommodation is provided for more than six guests and/or staff, or such accommodation is provided above the first floor or below the ground floor, a **Fire Certificate** granted by the **Fire Authority** will be required.

At 15 Back Street, Surfbourne, the accommodation is on only the ground and first floors. Since not more than six guests are catered for and no staff live in, a Fire Certificate is not required.

All the other hotels we have looked at sleep more than six guests, and therefore require Fire Certificates. At The Belfry, where the guest accommodation is on three floors, a Fire Certificate would be needed even if the number of guests did not exceed six.

As to the requirements before a certificate is granted, much depends on how simply, or otherwise, the premises are laid out. It is worth noting that different Fire Authorities interpret the legislation in different ways. If there are any doubts in your mind, the local **Fire Safety Advisor** should be consulted at the earliest opportunity.

At a minimum, the following must be provided to obtain a Fire Certificate:

FIRE ROUTINE

1. If you discover a fire, Break the Glass.

2. If you hear the fire alarm, leave the building by the nearest exit. (Don't use lifts.)

Fig. 3. Notice for display at fire alarm callpoints in public areas.

FIRE ROUTINE

1. If you discover a fire immediately raise the alarm. The nearest alarm callpoint to your room is [*at the top of the staircase next to Room number 2* . . .]

2. On hearing the fire alarm (a continuously ringing bell) leave the building via the nearest available escape route and assemble at [*the front lawn* . . .]

3. Do not use the lift/s.

4. Do not stop to collect personal belongings.

5. Do no re-enter the building until told it is safe to do so.

N.B. Make yourself familiar with the escape routes from the building NOW.

Fig. 4. Fire notice for display in guest bedrooms.

- a fire alarm system
- fire extinguishers (of the type approved locally)
- a secondary lighting system
- fire resisting and self-closing internal doors.

In addition, further installations, *eg* a fire escape, may be specified, notices must be displayed in bedrooms to tell guests what to do if a fire is discovered, and all equipment must be regularly inspected and serviced and the results recorded.

The type of notice that should be displayed in bedrooms and at callpoints is shown in Figures 3 and 4.

Although it is not necessary to have a Fire Certificate providing application has been made for one, it should be remembered that the refusal of a certificate, perhaps after a period has been allowed for work to be carried out, will effectively close the premises. On the plus side, once a certificate has been granted it cannot be revoked by the imposition of new provisions, *but see below*.

Exit signs need to conform to the **Health & Safety (Safety Signs and Signals) Regulations 1996**. Your local **Fire Safety Advisor** will advise.

Still on the subject of fire safety, regulations regarding fire retardant standards for furniture and furnishings are constantly under review. Currently, the **Furniture and Furnishings (Fire) (Safety) Regulations 1988 (as amended)** do not apply to hotels in general though the **Fire Safety Advisor** may require part of that legislation to be applied. However, if hotels and the like are used other than for the normal shortstay type of business, *eg* as a 'House of Multiple Occupancy' (usually where the guests are using the hotel as their home) these regulations do apply and could involve a hotelier having to replace all or most of the furniture.

If you employ anyone, the **Fire Precautions (Workplace) Regulations 1997** (as amended in 1999) may, depending on the result of current negotiations, require you to assess fire risks and additional requirements may be imposed by the **Fire Safety Advisor**. As always, seek professional advice before committing yourself.

Food Regulations
When carrying on *any* form of business involving food, the premises are subject to the provisions of the **Food Safety (General Food Hygiene) Regulations 1995** and the **Food Safety (Temperature Control) Regulations 1995**. The relevant Act of Parliament is the **Food Safety Act 1990**, the most important aim of which is to ensure that all food produced for sale is safe to eat. It also requires descriptions to be accurate.

Included in the main regulations are:

- The premises — its construction, sanitary and handwashing facilities, ventilation, lighting, drainage, and changing facilities.

- Food preparation, *etc* — the maintenance, cleaning and disinfecting of rooms used.

- The equipment — cleaning and disinfecting. (Anti-bacterial agents must be used to reinforce the cleaning process.)

- Personal hygiene — the necessity for personal cleanliness and wearing of protective clothing where appropriate.

- The food — its handling and washing, plus the temperature at which certain foods must be kept, also disposal of waste.

- The water supply — adequate *drinking* water to be available and used for making ice.

The Industry Guide to Good Hygiene Practice: Catering Guide (ISBN 0 900 103 00 0) gives detailed advice on the interpretation and application of these regulations.

Assessing risk is now a requirement for nearly all aspects of your business (see pages 106–7). With the help of booklets obtainable from your local **EHO (Environmental Health Officer),** you must identify and control potential food hazards under HACCP (Hazard Analysis Critical Control Point).

EHOs of the local authority police the regulations. They have power to enter all relevant premises to detect offences and frequently arrive unannounced.

If premises are found to be an imminent risk to health, they may be closed on the issue of an emergency prohibition notice. This could mean the end of your livelihood.

Swingeing fines and/or imprisonment can be imposed on conviction for each of the most serious offences.

Regulations are quite rightly being tightened all the time. The result of compliance is safer food for your guests and freedom from actions against you, which might include civil claims for the effects of food poisoning.

For the first time ever, *all* hotel-type premises with four or more letting bedrooms now have to be registered with the local authority. If starting from scratch, four weeks' notice needs to be given before opening so that an enforcement officer can visit and advise on hygiene.

A booklet *The Food Safety Act 1990 and You* can be obtained from Food Sense, London SE99 7TT Tel: 0645 556000. It is also obtainable from the Environmental Health Department of the local authority, as are leaflets explaining the main provisions of the food regulations including identifying and controlling hazards. Additionally, many EHOs issue notes for guidance to hoteliers.

It would be unwise to commit yourself to buying a hotel where much work needs to be done to bring it up to food safety standards, without accounting for such work in the price you are prepared to pay.

Other legislation

Hotel operations are governed by a number of other Acts of Parliament, each of which will be dealt with in the appropriate section. A list of such legislation is provided at the end of the book. Planning law, which must be strictly adhered to in every case, is dealt with under the next heading.

CAN WE USE OUR EXISTING RESIDENCE?

If your house is large enough and is in the right place (estate agents say there are only three things to consider — location, location and location), you may wish to consider taking paying guests, so avoiding the need to move.

Ask yourself, if any of your neighbours wanted to take paying guests, would you object to the prospect of increased traffic, noise, *etc*?

Most premises where there is a change of use require planning permission. Do your groundwork very thoroughly. Make sure by reference to the title deeds of your house that its use as a hotel is not prohibited. Then work out what accommodation you want to retain for your own use and how much you plan to give over for guests.

Before going any further, it would be wise to make out a sketch plan for each floor and then to seek the informal advice of your local authority planning department.

Incidentally, planning permission is required for every sign which is not within the curtilage of your property and for most that are.

If all appears straightforward check whether a Fire Certificate is required. If so, what work will need to be carried out? The local **Fire Safety Advisor** will advise. And since the Food Safety Act covers *all* businesses concerned with handling food, how much work will need to be done to your kitchen to bring it within the regulations? The expert is the EHO of your local authority.

A word of warning. A private house can rarely be converted into a hotel of any size without substantial costly alterations. It may yet be worth it if everything else is favourable. If it is necessary to raise capital, see Chapter 4 for details.

Buying for conversion

The considerations applying to using your existing residence also apply here to a large extent, including, of course, planning permission. The advantages may include:

● a carefully chosen location
● an interior designed to your own tastes and needs.

THE GOING CONCERN

This is the most common way of buying into the business and in most cases is advantageous for a number of reasons:

● The hotel will already be known.
● The layout will be purpose built or already adapted.
● No planning permission for change of use will be required.
● A Fire Certificate, if required, will have been obtained.
● Approvals for work carried out will have been obtained.
● If a bar exists, a liquor licence will be in force.
● You can start trading as soon as you move in.

When viewing properties, it will pay to ensure that all necessary approvals have in fact been obtained.

Sources of information

The magazine most widely known for advertising hotels for sale is *Daltons Weekly*. Not only is there a section for private advertisers, but most of the main business transfer agents use it extensively.

Other nationally available magazines worth attention are:

● *Caterer and Hotelkeeper* (weekly).
● *Hotel and Restaurant Magazine* (monthly).

In addition, if you are intending to search in a specific area, the local **Hotels Association** (details obtainable from the **Tourist Information Centre**) may be able to help. As well as supplying you with the particulars of local agents and regional newspapers and magazines in which 'hotels for sale' advertisements appear, you may be told of hotels currently on the market.

Having decided in broad terms what you are looking for, write down your requirements and register with a selection of agents. (Solicitors in Scotland are widely involved in estate agency work.) Bear in mind that the more you register with, the more you will have to correspond with when you have found what you're looking for. Failure to cancel your name from registers may mean details being forwarded to you for the foreseeable future! Since properties are usually filed in order of price, remember to let agents know the most you can pay.

To ensure a steady stream of material arriving on your doormat, arrange for local publications (if searching in specific areas) to be sent to you. Your newsagent can often make the necessary arrangements.

Sifting and filing the literature
There could rapidly be hundreds of sets of property details cascading through your letter box. This is when you will find a ring binder, a paper punch and a large waste paper bin useful.

A lot of what arrives will be totally unsuited to your needs, for various reasons. These should be immediately consigned to the bin to avoid confusion.

If you have a definite area in mind, you will obviously only keep details of properties within that region. Otherwise, divide the sets of details into areas *eg* South West, and subdivide into counties within that area. Using your own code, mark up each topsheet as a 'probable' or a 'possible'. If you really want to go to town, have two binders, one for each category.

As more details arrive and you add them to your stock, sift and reject until you are able to identify a short list. How many in each short list will depend on how urgent your search is, how much resolve you have to hold out for something as near perfect as possible, and how much time you can devote to carrying out the search.

Freehold or leasehold?
Most of the sets of details you receive will be for **freehold** properties. This means you are being invited to buy in exactly the same way as you would buy a private house.

The advantages are clear:

- Within reason and subject to any necessary permissions you can tailor the premises to your needs, adding as required.
- The asset will appreciate in value over the years.

The disadvantages are perhaps not so clear:

* You may be putting all your eggs in one basket.
* You may need to borrow more than you would prefer.
* You may find the hotel difficult to sell if the business fails.

Some of the properties coming your way will be **leasehold**. This means you are effectively being invited to rent a property which will almost certainly never become yours. Short leases, with less than five years to run, should be dismissed out of hand. The longer the lease, the better.

The *one* advantage with leasehold property is the price, which will be considerably less than freehold. This may enable you to:

* Buy into a better (and possibly more profitable) hotel than would otherwise be the case.
* Avoid excessive (or any) borrowing.
* Maybe retain another property while leasing this one.

The disadvantages are:

* A lease is generally a declining asset.
* You will not be able to alter the hotel as you might wish.
* Valuations of leases, even by professionals, can be wildly inaccurate.
* Lenders are often not keen to lend without security.

Great care is necessary when buying any property, but particularly so with a leasehold one. An experienced commercial conveyancing solicitor is essential to get the terms of the lease right before you even think of signing anything. Such a solicitor will negotiate the best terms for you, *eg* your repairing liabilities, and will ensure you sign only when those terms, which will include covenants, are not detrimental to your interests.

Remember that it is by no means certain the lease will be renewed at the end of its normal life.

The biggest snag with leasing property is that under the **Law of Property Act 1925** your obligations do not cease when you sell on the lease. This means you could be successfully sued for any rent arrears and other liabilities until the lease runs out (or until the Act is repealed), even though you may have sold it years earlier.

As a general rule, leasing hotel property is riddled with pitfalls. **Expert advice is essential**.

Preparing your strategy

To look at two or three properties a day is perhaps ideal, depending on how far apart they are.

Staying at one of them incognito will give you a view from the inside as opposed to what a vendor might want to show you.

Most properties come onto the market at the end of the season, with most completions before the new season starts. Nevertheless, circumstances bring hotels onto the market at all times of the year and if you are searching in a busy period you will probably need to book your overnight stay. If not, and the hotel is open, arrive unannounced and stay only if the property has possibilities as far as you are concerned. Don't miss the opportunity to arrive on spec at a better proposition. Be armed with notebook and pen.

Allow as much time as you can for return visits, if necessary. Any spare time can be used in reconnoitring the area and finding sources of information, as indicated later on. Don't be surprised if no one knows the property is on the market.

In any event, vendors will not want their guests to know they are selling. It undermines confidence. Many will not even tell their staff. It has been known for quite senior staff to know nothing until a new owner has taken over and gets mistaken for a guest on entering the dining room!

Vendors will want to arrange appointments to view when no one is around, often after the lunchtime period. The earlier part of the day can then be used to view other properties from the outside. Some agents are very adept at taking photographs to exclude the smoking factory chimney next door! Keep making copious notes. Memories fade fast and it is easy to get properties mixed up.

WHAT SHOULD WE LOOK OUT FOR?

Never miss an opportunity to make notes.

- If you had to make a booking, how did you get dealt with on the telephone? Would *you* have done it that way?
- How easy was it for you to find the hotel? Could it be made easier?
- What were your first impressions? Did it make you want to go inside? Could anything be done to improve it?
- What sort of reception did you get when you arrived? Did it make you feel comfortable? Would *you* do it differently?
- If you arrived on spec, were you impressed when you asked to look at a room?
- What sort of service were you given? Were you offered a tray of tea?

Was your case carried for you? How could the service be improved?

- Did the inside strike you as welcoming? Did it make you want to stay? Could you live there? Could it be improved?

- Were the facilities what you would expect from a hotel of this type? Could you improve on them?

- What standard of food was served? Was it as good as you expected? Would you do it that way?

- Were the tables attractively laid out? What was the crockery and cutlery like? Was it clean? How about the prongs of the forks? Were you impressed, or otherwise?

- What was the table service like? Who did the waiting? Was the waiter clean and tidy? Were there areas for improvement?

- How full was the hotel? Was it reasonable for the time of year? Would *you* be happy with that level of trade?

These are but a few of the questions you should be continually asking yourself. Even if a property is not for you, make a note of what you have seen, the good as well as the bad. Apart from when you start operating yourself, this period should be the most beneficial in terms of learning.

Keeping appointments

As you may have found out when you were selling your house, nothing is more annoying or discourteous than people not turning up for an appointment.

If you haven't had the opportunity to view earlier from the outside, and you realise on seeing the property for the first time it is not for you, still go in armed with your notebook and list of questions. You needn't spend too long inside but be surprised if you don't learn something. Keep notebook in hand and write to increase your knowledge whenever something interesting strikes you.

Needless to say, the quantity you write will depend on whether you are seriously considering purchasing. Or maybe by this time you have got the bit between your teeth and want to know just about everything! Never be afraid to ask questions. Be direct — that doesn't mean be rude — but persist until you have received an answer that satisfies you. If the vendor has got skeletons in the cupboard, do your best to find out about them before the cupboard becomes yours along with the rest of the property.

Points to look for

A few suggestions of what you might ask, notebook and pen poised, though not necessarily the moment you step across the threshold:

- How long have you been here?
- Why are you selling? (Follow up as necessary.)
- How profitable is the business?
- Are you registered for VAT?
- Do you have the accounts for the last six years? (Less if the trading period has been shorter.)
- Do you hold a Fire Certificate? (It must, by law, be kept on the premises.)
- Do you hold a drinks licence, if so what sort?
- How many guests can you take?
- How many are staying at the moment?
- Do you cater for non-residents?
- How long do you keep open?
- How many staff do you employ?
- What do they do?
- Do they know you're selling?
- What advertising do you do?
- Where do you get most response?
- Which area(s) do most of your guests come from?
- What advance bookings do you have?
- What gradings do you have?
- By whom has your hotel been inspected?
- When did an Environmental Health Officer last visit?
- What heating system do you have?
- Have you built any extensions or made substantial alterations? (Should be shown on the plan attached to the Fire Certificate.)
- Did you obtain planning and/or other necessary permissions?
- Is any of the furniture or equipment not your own property?
- May I have a brochure and tariff?

You will no doubt think of other questions to ask but these should put you on the right track. Try not to give the impression you are applying the third degree but do not let the vendor duck questions like a politician!

Accounts will be looked at in detail in Chapter 7. Suffice it to say for the present that by law they must be kept for six years. An on-the-ball vendor will probably have run off copies of the last year's accounts for those who appear seriously interested.

That same vendor may, however, have made the accounts look attractive in order to trap a buyer. It is a ploy that is far from unknown. At a cursory glance, the accounts should show a turnover that has steadily increased over the years. Sudden fluctuations need explanation and will certainly be queried by an experienced accountant.

You will recall that accounts of limited companies have to be audited; not so with other types of ownership. Since it is normal for Inland Revenue staff to have a heavy workload, not every set of accounts submitted (or set of figures for small businesses) which seems to warrant queries can be questioned. It is therefore quite easy for a dishonest vendor to make out that a business is more profitable than it really is in order to sell it.

On the subject of dishonest hoteliers, beware those who excuse a lowish turnover by saying, with a nod and a wink, that they don't tell the tax man everything. Some are stupid enough to confide this to a total stranger — you could well be a tax inspector!

If vendors give you the impression they are being less than honest over any aspect of their business, the chance is they are being dishonest over other things as well. Avoid them like the plague!

While you are looking around, watch out for furniture and equipment which are on their last legs; a lot of money can be involved. Write furiously in your notebook. List *every* item of kitchen equipment and have your list ready for when the subject is studied in detail in Chapter 6. You will be amazed how some hoteliers operate with little, or in some cases, no commercial equipment. Also note what arrangements, if any, have been made for guests' use of a telephone.

If you get a chance, look under a bed or two, run your finger along the tops of doors, look in drawers and cupboards. If nothing else, it will tell you something about the staff.

Three more items for your notebook:

- In hotels with four or more bedrooms (or eight or more bedspaces), is the tariff displayed at the entrance or at reception? (See page 100.)

- Is a notice under the **Business Names Act 1985** displayed? (See page 87.)

- In a bar, is there a notice under the **Weights and Measures Acts** and is there a bar price list displayed? (See page 150.)

If you think you might be seriously interested, don't jump in and appear too eager; there is far too much at stake. Ask if you may return, perhaps the next day when you have had a chance to think things through.

Analyse what you have written down and compile another list of questions, to include if they have any objection to a full structural survey and approaches by your accountant. Also ask whether they have made any claims on their insurance or if any special conditions have been applied to the policy.

WHAT TO DO AFTER SELECTING A PROPERTY

Having decided you would like to investigate further, the question of price will be uppermost in your mind.

It is normal for a hotel to be sold fully equipped, so you can trade immediately. That is the theory! However, there is no need for you to buy what would be more at home in a rubbish skip. Note what you don't want and, as discussed in Chapter 6, assess what replacement items will cost you so that you can consider adjusting the price should you eventually make an offer.

Your own accommodation will normally be sold unfurnished. It will therefore be unnecessary to dispose of everything that is currently furnishing your own house; another good reason for having your own rooms as spacious as possible.

If you haven't yet obtained copies of the accounts, ask for them now, as many years as are available. Your accountant will want to study them.

Another thing your accountant will want to know is how the asking price is made up. There are normally three elements:

- property
- goodwill
- fixtures and fittings.

The apportionment to each is known as the 'split'. The size of the first two elements is significant in the calculation of Capital Gains Tax. Everyone's circumstances are different, so no general guidelines are appropriate.

Goodwill is a traditional element of the price and is calculated on the past performance of the business. A rule of thumb sometimes applied is the sum of two years' net profits. It is, however, there to be negotiated, and generally the vendor will prefer the figure to be high, the buyer low.

Any generalisations can be changed by individual circumstances. It is essential, therefore, to seek the advice of an experienced accountant. Take a note of the name, address and telephone number of the vendor's accountant and solicitor and leave details of your own.

Don't feel you have to rush things. Maybe you have still to finalise the sale of your house. Make steady progress to show you are serious but don't rush headlong into something you may regret. It is not a good thing, whether or not you have viewed through an agent, to discuss price at this stage. If you had felt the property was grossly overpriced, you wouldn't be viewing it. You still have much to do.

Selecting a professional advisor

To help you with what could be the most important decision of your life, you will need good professional advice.

Accountants, solicitors and surveyors

There are good, bad and dishonest in every profession, including accountants, solicitors and surveyors. Your object must be to avoid the minority who are inept and/or unprincipled.

Each professional advisor you choose should belong to one of the nationally recognised professional bodies, *eg* the Institute of Chartered Accountants or the Royal Institution of Chartered Surveyors. With solicitors and accountants you can work on the principle that the larger the firm, the greater the range of advice and facilities offered and, in consequence, the higher the charges. If you are looking purely for advice on 'the split' and the viability of your intended purchase, and for book-keeping advice leading to the preparation and submission of your accounts to the Inland Revenue, a small firm would be the one to go for. Similarly, a small firm of solicitors should be able to advise you on all conveyancing matters. The lease, however, may be a different matter.

Professional advisors generally fight within certain parameters to get you the best deal. If, for example, a particular restricting covenant favouring the vendor is normal in a contract, your solicitor may well not mention it if the other side doesn't. Whereas some might consider it wrong to suggest that the deal you get is only as good as your professional advisor, work on that principle and you won't go far wrong.

Do not be duped into thinking an advisor is as good as the firm's advertisement in *Yellow Pages*. It could be argued that, with enough personal recommendations and a good local reputation, flamboyant advertisements should be unnecessary.

When looking for a surveyor, you should contact one on the personal recommendation of a couple of hoteliers who have used the service recently. Check what the charge is going to be and see if you can be there at the time of inspection. Being shown what needs attention will help you enormously to understand the written report when you receive it.

If you already have solicitors, the firm may be able to recommend an accountant, and so on. Your bank manager may also help you to compile a short list.

Write to each of the professional advisors and ask if they would be prepared to meet you to discuss your needs, what their charges are and whether there is any fee for an initial chat. Most will give you an interview without charge, but it is important to ask the question. One intending hotelier met an accountant over a pint in the local pub and received a bill for the consultation!

Unless the firm has been recommended by more than one hotelier, ask how many small hotels are on their books, how long they have been in business locally and to what extent a qualified person will deal personally with your affairs. Never be afraid to ask direct questions. If you don't, people are often left in doubt as to what you want to know.

Look for prompt replies from solicitors and accountants. All business people, particularly if there's a chance of getting new business, should deal with correspondence promptly. Does the reply give the impression the writer is business-like without being stuffy?

If you have any reservations at all, do not pursue matters with that advisor. You need to have confidence in the person you eventually see. Even then, don't be afraid to say 'no'. Unless you emerge from an interview feeling that you have found someone who is competent, who you can talk to comfortably, who will fight as hard as is necessary to get you a good deal, and whose charges are as reasonable as you can expect, it is better to keep looking.

Local Hotels Associations
The local Hotels Association may also help, in the hope that if you eventually buy in the area you will become a member. If not in the telephone directory, its address and number will be supplied from the **Tourist Information Centre**. The person who runs it may even know why the hotel you are enquiring about is up for sale.

Many of the members are themselves proprietors of small hotels, some of them 'rookies' who have recently gone through what you are striving to achieve. They will be only too pleased to pass on their experiences and to recommend (or otherwise) a professional advisor.

Insurance brokers
You may be able to save yourself time and money at this stage by calling on a local insurance broker. This is imperative if the hotel you are looking at is anywhere near the sea or water of any kind. The vendor will hardly tell you if there is a history of flooding or, worse

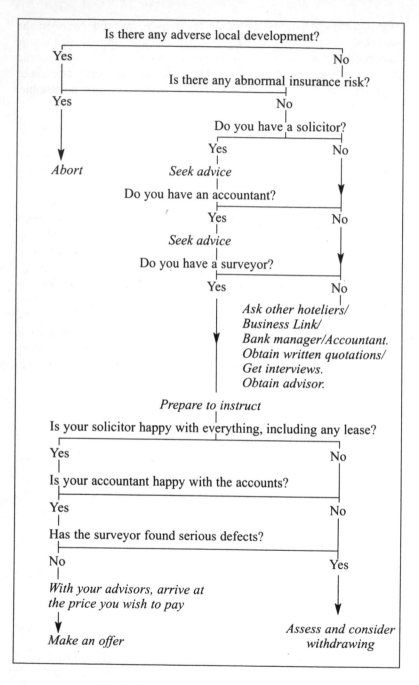

Fig. 5. What to do after selecting a property.

still, subsidence. That could be the real reason the property is on the market.

A good broker will offer you every assistance in the hope of getting your business in due course and will ask you questions in an attempt to find out if there is any extraordinary risk. If the risk seems unacceptable, you may need to start looking again.

Local authority planning departments
If you are still harbouring doubts as to why the property has come on the market, a visit to the planning department of the local authority can put your mind at rest (or otherwise).

There you will be able to discover if there are any planning applications current for the surrounding area and, if so, to inspect the actual applications and drawings submitted with it. All **Planning Registers** must by law be open to the public and current policy is that there is no charge.

The **Local Plan**, also available for inspection, will pinpoint any future planned development. It could be to your advantage. It could spell ruin.

Should you be unable to visit during office hours, a letter with a site plan and the property highlighted in red will elicit whether there are any current applications which might have a detrimental effect on the area in the future.

Taking the next step
Once you have satisfied yourself that:

- there are no abnormal insurance risks
- no detrimental local development is planned
- the property is structurally sound

discuss the value with the surveyor.

Armed with his opinion and your own calculations as to what needs to be spent on furniture, alterations, *etc*, next:

- Discuss the accounts, 'the split' and the asking price with your accountant.
- If so advised, obtain an independent audit and valuation of the business.

- Discuss the question of price with your solicitor.
- Discuss the lease, if applicable, with your solicitor.
- Arrive at the price you are prepared to pay.
- Never pay more than the asking price.
- Never get involved in gazumping.
- Make a firm offer.

CHECKLIST

Have you. . .

- Informed business transfer agents of your requirements?
- Ordered local newspapers to be sent to you?
- Made arrangements to receive specialist magazines?
- Made yourself conversant with relevant legislation?
- Decided on freehold or leasehold?
- Arranged your strategy for viewing?
- Prepared a list of questions to ask?
- Got a good idea what properties are worth?
- Viewed and assessed what extra funds, if any, you will need?
- Made satisfactory local enquiries?
- Sought appropriate professional advice?
- Indicated you are seriously interested in buying?
- Made a firm offer?

4

Raising Capital

Having selected your intended property and estimated what money you will need, you may now need to borrow — but how much? The time has come to assess your needs carefully.

SOURCES OF FINANCE

Your own resources

These will have to be significant. As has been said before, you will be lucky to come across any lender, and certainly not a reputable one, who is prepared to advance money for your business venture unless you are committing funds yourself.

At this stage, unless you have other money available, it will be expected that you have either sold your house, or at least have the sale well under way. If the latter, by the reaction you have received you will know within reason the amount you will end up with. Allow generously for the various fees you will have to pay, such as estate agents, solicitors and removals.

Add to the net amount any savings you may have: redundancy money; life assurance policies which have matured or which you have chosen to cash in; stocks and shares; the proceeds of anything you have decided to sell; any tax rebates due. You will arrive at a figure known as your capital.

Private loans

Loans from friends or relatives to make up any shortfall between your capital and what you may need to pay out are generally not a good idea. People fall out and then get spiteful. The untimely calling in of an informal loan could put your business in jeopardy.

If you *have* to borrow from friends or relatives, insist on the terms being drawn up by a solicitor and ensure you are given adequate notice if demands are made for the loan to be repaid. Would you want to lend a friend money without the loan being formalised by a solicitor? See pages 38–9 regarding partnerships.

Banks

One of the large banks is the most-used port of call for people like you starting a business. If you have had a bank account for some time and are entirely happy with the way in which it is run, you may now reap the benefit if you discussed your plans with the manager earlier. It is an excellent thing to get a bank business manager on your side.

Competition between the banks to capture a large slice of the small business market is fierce, and each puts together a very useful and informative **business start-up pack**.

Unless you are perfectly satisfied with your own bank and are convinced the business manager will cater for all your needs, call in at a number of banks and ask for a business pack. See how you are dealt with, the degree of help offered at this early stage, and the attractions of each bank for you.

The types of loan, the amounts offered, interest rates, arrangement fees and the terms for repayment vary widely. All business accounts attract considerable charges (more of this later) and it may suit your purpose to opt for banks which offer the first one or two year's banking free — but watch out for conditions you may not be able to meet. See what each bank offers you.

Although with modern technology it is unnecessary to bank locally, it is an advantage to be able to pop in and see your manager. He may well know your type of business, if not the actual one, and may be able to offer you useful advice. Unofficially, of course, very welcome business may be put your way.

Building societies

Where your own living accommodation forms part of the premises, as is usual in a small hotel, some building societies offer commercial mortgages. When borrowers are few, lenders often extend the scope of their normal lending and offer competitive rates. Make enquiries at a number of societies, see what they have to offer and if their rates, charges and so on compare favourably with those offered by banks.

Other lenders

It will rarely be a good idea to approach finance houses. Because they borrow the money before lending it out and then have to make a profit, interest rates are often high. It has also been known for some to lend money without the borrower having any capital. Any business which is financed 100 per cent, particularly when interest rates are high, is doomed to failure.

Low-interest loans, assistance and training may be available in former coal mining and steel producing areas. Grants may also be available in what are left of **Enterprise Zones**. The Department of the Environment on (020) 7890 3755 will tell you where the **Enterprise Zones** are. Under the **Development of Tourism Act 1969** the Wales Tourist Board can offer grants for certain projects. A word of caution, however. Do not rely on obtaining a grant (as opposed to a loan). There are very few around.

Government-sponsored schemes

These are always liable to change and the facilities available vary from area to area. A good source of information initially are **Business Links** which work in conjunction with **Training and Enterprise Councils (TECs)**. They can be described as DTI-sponsored one-stop shops for business advice and guidance, much of which is free. All must meet criteria laid down by the DTI. To find your local office, telephone the Business Link Signposting Line on 08457 567765. The **Scottish Business Shop Network** on 0800 787878, **Wales Business Connect** on 0345 969798, and **LEDU** (Northern Ireland) on (01232) 491031 perform similar functions outside England.

In addition, there are **Enterprise Agencies** in many areas. They are sponsored locally with funding from large companies as well as local government, and offer assistance, again much of it free, to new and existing businesses. Business Link will tell you if there is an Enterprise Agency in your area.

TYPES OF LOANS

Commercial mortgages

This is a long-term loan for properties where living accommodation forms part of the premises. At one time such loans were offered only through building societies but are now available from a number of banks. The criteria vary but, as with a domestic mortgage, security is required.

Depending on the lender's current rules, up to three years 'holiday' from capital repayments may be offered. Interest rates, which may be variable or fixed, are often negotiable.

Overdrafts

Although a bank may offer an overdraft as a normal facility to help balance the books, it is often short-term to cater for a special contingency or to buy, perhaps, a new piece of equipment.

The interest rate will fluctuate with the bank base rate. The worst aspect of an overdraft is that it is repayable on demand. Are you prepared to take the risk of having to repay when it might not be convenient? Under no circumstances should an account be allowed to go into overdraft without a manager's specific permission. Not only will the interest rate be sky-high but it will erode any confidence the manager may have in you.

Other types of loan

Banks will offer business loans under various names. Each scheme has its advantages and disadvantages and what will suit one client will not suit another. Your object should be to 'tailor' a scheme to your particular needs. Study all the literature provided to decide which is best for you. Not only can you discuss the subject with the manager but your accountant, local Enterprise Agency or Business Link can offer expert advice.

If you find you do not have the track record a bank may require, or, perhaps, you cannot provide the requisite security, you may be eligible to apply for the **Loan Guarantee Scheme**. If your proposal meets the prevailing criteria, part of the loan is guaranteed by the government in return for a premium. Banks can supply you with details of how to apply.

MAKING A BUSINESS PROPOSAL

Banks provide forms to help you give the detailed information required in a business proposal or, as it is sometimes called, a **business plan**. Every responsible lender will expect you to be able to justify your eligibility for a loan and it is the business plan that imposes the discipline on you to:

- set out your objectives
- see if your proposals are viable
- convince a lender his investment is justified
- show you can service (pay back) a loan.

It is not a document you can complete in five minutes. It will need very careful research before you even start to fill it in. If you should find the task daunting, you may wish to seek the advice of your accountant or Business Link. Do bear in mind, however, there is a lot of paperwork involved in running a business, particularly if you employ staff and/or are registered for VAT, so it would be as well to at least make a start on your own.

Even if you do not need to borrow money, you will still need your hotel to make a profit. Completing a business plan will give you an awareness of how your finances should be structured. Look upon the plan from the point of view of someone being asked to invest substantially in a business venture. Once it is complete, would it convince **you** it is a project you should put **your** hard-earned cash into and, if it failed, would you get your money back?

Presenting your case

Whether or not you use a lender's form, the following is a guide to the type of information you need to supply:

- the name, address, date of birth, academic and/or professional qualifications of the principals
- your exact financial situation
- details of the business you are setting up/acquiring
- your reasons for going into business and the relevant experience of the principals
- your intentions to acquire any necessary skills
- the date you intend to start
- your long-term objectives
- details of staff to be employed and/or retained
- how your tariff will be structured
- what competition there is
- who your potential customers are
- the advantage, if any, your hotel has over the competition
- your proposals for improvement
- your advertising intentions
- details of existing equipment including life expectancy; new equipment required and the cost
- your setting up costs
- your profit and loss budget forecast
- your cashflow projection
- your borrowing requirement.

Once you have completed your proposal, it should show your intended lender that:

- you fully understand what you are letting yourself in for
- you are capable of running a business successfully
- you have, or intend to obtain, the necessary skills
- your objectives are sound
- there is a market for your service
- the proposed business will make a profit
- you are able to service a loan
- you are committing your own money to the venture
- there is sufficient security in the event of failure.

As you have seen, profit and cashflow forecasts are required to complete your business plan. These are best completed on forms supplied by lenders and vary from bank to bank.

CASE STUDY

To help understand what is required, take a look at the case of Andrew and Christine Bright, a married couple who intend to buy the Bourne Hotel at Surfbourne.

Andrew is 50 and has recently been made redundant from the Tessa Oil Company as Personnel Manager.

In his 20 years with the company, which he joined after completing a short service commission in the RAF, he gained experience of book-keeping and latterly supervised a staff of 26. His knowledge of staff matters and accounts will help him with the hotel's bookwork and to manage the four part-time staff.

His educational qualifications include two A-levels in French and German. He feels his language skills will help him with the increasing number of foreign tourists visiting the area.

Christine, aged 47, is working a month's notice with a firm of solicitors where she is employed as a legal secretary on a salary of £18,000 pa. Her education included one A-level in Business Studies. She is a competent cook and feels capable of preparing food of a good standard for around 20 guests.

They have viewed the Bourne Hotel twice, have made copious notes regarding the facilities and equipment, and have been given a copy of the accounts for the last three years. These show a turnover of £95,419 including VAT (£81,208 net) derived from seasonal trading from March to October. They feel they can do much better.

The VAT-inclusive tariff for bed, breakfast and evening meal is based on £34 per person per night in rooms without en suite bathroom, and £38 with sea view and en suite bathroom. A ten per cent reduction is made for weekly bookings, and outside June, July, August and September a 20 per cent reduction applies irrespective of the length of stay.

Once they are committed to the purchase, they will take advantage of free counselling at the local Business Link where advice will be given on their various projections and plans before they put a firm proposal to the bank. They will need to take along all documents in their possession which relate to their financial position.

They will also be able to get free part-time training in the various aspects of running a business. It is their intention to run the hotel for approximately ten years before taking early retirement.

As required by law (see Chapter 6) they will take
but will dispense with the washer-up on acquirir
washer. They have noted that three new items of
will be required at the outset and have costed th_
catering equipment suppliers.

Until they get settled they will adopt the existing tariff to enc_
regular guests to return and will keep to existing advertising patterns.
They already consider the facilities superior to most offered by other
hotels in the town, but intend to upgrade to all en suite accommodation
after the first year. To help with funding for this project, they will open
over Christmas and the New Year.

Assessing borrowing requirements

In order to find out what sort of financing they will require, they first
have to look at their current capital situation.

Assets:		
	Sale of house (net of fees and mortgage)	£185,000
	Other capital (inc. redundancy payment)	£68,000
	TOTAL	£253,000

Since the Bourne Hotel almost exactly meets their requirements, they
are inclined to offer the asking price of £300,000 subject to a satisfactory
surveyor's report and the advice of their accountant. Not wanting to
commit all their capital, they have discussed asking for a loan of
£65,000.

On this basis, their start-up costs must come out of the balance of
£18,000. At first glance, this seems more than adequate. How will it
stand up after a **Start-Up Costs Chart** has been prepared?

Although some items must be assumed, reasonably accurate figures
can be prepared by asking questions.

For example, the Brights were strongly recommended to an accountant through the local Hotels Association. When they telephoned and
stated their possible requirements, they were quoted 'not more than
£200' to advise them initially and to get their accounts running. Further,
providing the firm was instructed to submit their accounts to the Inland
Revenue, they wouldn't be billed until the end of their financial year.

'Not more than £475' was quoted by two firms of local solicitors for
a straightforward conveyance plus £750 for a thorough survey. All fees
are subject to VAT and the solicitor and surveyor would require payment
immediately. They are awaiting replies to their written enquiries and
confirmation of fees before making a final choice.

A local firm of insurance brokers has offered a 'package' insurance

Start-Up Costs Chart

	£
Solicitor	560
Surveyor	900
Insurance	600
Membership fees & licences	300
Brochures, stationery, postage	550
Advertising (prepaid)	780
Finance/arrangement/legal fees	1450
Stock	520
Rates	465
	6125
Add purchase price	300,000
Total outlay	306,125
Deduct capital introduced	241,125
Loan required	65,000

Fig.6. Start-up costs chart.

policy specially drawn up by a well-known company for a number of hotels in the town and quoted an exact cost. (Insurance is dealt with in Chapter 5.)

Fees for membership of the local Hotels Association and a national organisation, together with the cost of all required licences, have been ascertained.

Two firms of printers have provided samples and quotes for an initial supply of brochures and stationery, to which an allowance of £20 for postage stamps has been added.

The vendor has already paid for tried and tested sources of advertising so there is no likely fall-off in bookings. The Brights will be invited to pay for this. (See also Chapter 8.)

The stock has been purposely reduced by the vendor and a price quoted, assuming the Brights decide to accept it. (Stock is dealt with in Chapter 5.)

Since the rates bills have already been paid, the purchasers will have to pay up front for that portion of rates applicable to the period they occupy the hotel in the current financial year. Once the moving in date has been suggested, this figure can be estimated with some accuracy.

Finally, their intended lender has estimated a sum for arrangement and legal fees in the event of their borrowing £65,000 by way of a commercial mortgage. An 'absolute maximum' figure should be shown here.

The whole makes up the Start-Up Costs Chart (Figure 6). It is always better to over-estimate than to show figures which prove inadequate.

The cashflow forecast

So a third of the Brights' remaining capital has been eroded on start-up costs. Since they are looking to move in near the beginning of January and the hotel is not due to open until March, how will they get on with only an estimated £1,500 in deposits coming in?

The seasonal business is always the most difficult to manage financially because of the peaks and troughs. Again, since the economic situation can substantially affect bookings, as can the weather, assumptions that may be wildly inaccurate have to be made.

You will see on the forecasts, each of which covers six months (Figures 7 and 8) that alongside the **budget column** there is one for the **actual figure**. It is obviously in your best interest to get the calculations as near to the actual as possible and, again, try not to over-estimate what is coming in.

Although the Brights might get a good idea of how the income is apportioned throughout the season if the vendor lets them examine the books, the standard way of estimating hotel **turnover** is to calculate the

	JANUARY Budget	JANUARY Actual	FEBRUARY Budget	FEBRUARY Actual	MARCH Budget	MARCH Actual	APRIL Budget	APRIL Actual	MAY Budget	MAY Actual	JUNE Budget	JUNE Actual	TOTALS Budget	TOTALS Actual
RECEIPTS														
Cash Sales	500		1000		6000		8500		9500		17000		42500	
Capital Introduced	6500		1500										8000	
TOTAL RECEIPTS	7000		2500		6000		8500		9500		17000		50500	
PAYMENTS														
Stock & Provisions	850		700		1000		2000		1700		3500		9750	
Salaries & Wages					2500		2250		2250		2250		9250	
Rates	465						250		250		250		1215	
Insurance	600												600	
Repairs & Renewals	100		50		50		50		50		50		350	
Heat & Light					600						600		1200	
Printing/postage/adverts	1350		500		50		50		600		50		2600	
Motor & Travel	40		30		30		30		200		40		370	
Telephone			500						250				750	
Professional fees	1440												1440	
Capital payments			1010				2400						3410	
Membership fees	300												300	
Bank interest					1625						1625		3250	
Finance/arr/legal fees	1450												1450	
VAT payable (refund)					(380)						4500		4120	
TOTAL PAYMENTS	6595		2790		5475		7030		5300		12865		40055	
NET CASHFLOW	405		(290)		525		1470		4200		4135			
OPENING BANK BALANCE			405		115		640		2110		6310			
CLOSING BANK BALANCE	405		115		640		2110		6310		10445			

Fig. 7. Cashflow forecast for the Bourne Hotel, January to June.

	JULY	AUGUST	SEPTEMBER	OCTOBER	NOVEMBER	DECEMBER	ANNUAL TOTALS
RECEIPTS	Budget Actual	Budget Actual	Budget Actual	Budget Actual	Budget Actual	Budget Actual	Budget Actual
Cash Sales	17500	18000	16000	6000	500	7000	107500
Capital Introduced							8000
TOTAL RECEIPTS	17500	18000	16000	6000	500	7000	115500
PAYMENTS							
Stock & Provisions	3500	3500	3000	1200	150	1400	22500
Salaries & Wages	2650	2650	2650	2250	4000	2000	25450
Rates	250	250	250	250	250	250	2715
Insurance	50	50	50		50	50	600
Repairs & Renewals				250			850
Heat & Light		700	900			600	2700
Printing/postage/adverts	50	540	50		1100	200	4700
Motor & Travel	40		40	40	30	40	1100
Telephone		250			250		1250
Professional fees							1440
Capital payments							3410
Membership fees							300
Bank interest			1625			1625	6500
Finance/arr/legal fees							1450
VAT payable (refund)			7000			1500	12620
TOTAL PAYMENTS	6540	7940	15565	3990	5830	7665	87585
NET CASHFLOW	10960	10060	435	2010	(5330)	(665)	27915
OPENING BANK BALANCE	10445	21405	31465	31900	33910	28580	
CLOSING BANK BALANCE	21405	31465	31900	33910	28580	27915	

Fig. 8. Cashflow forecast for the Bourne Hotel, July to December.

percentage of bedspaces that will be filled at various times. From the tariff it can then be seen what the likely income will be.

For **The Bourne Hotel** with 20 bedspaces, it has been estimated that on average the hotel will be 75 per cent full during the 17 weeks of June, July, August and September. This gives a turnover inclusive of VAT, an allowance for bar takings and earlier deposits, of £68,500. Allowing for 40 per cent occupancy in the 17 weeks of March, April, May and October, a turnover of about £30,000 should be realised and a 100 per cent occupancy (with an increased tariff) in the week over Christmas and the New Year should produce £7,000.

It will be seen that in February, in order to keep the bank balance in the black, a further £1,500 of capital has had to be introduced.

Since **VAT** has to be paid with payments, all the 'payments' figures include this tax. The mechanics are explained in Chapter 7, but suffice it to say here that for those who are VAT registered the return which reconciles the difference between what is collected and what is paid out is normally submitted only once a quarter.

Andrew and Christine Bright were able to see how much was paid out in **provisions** from the vendor's accounts. Unless your tariff is exceptionally high or low, around 20 per cent of turnover is normal.

Since they are taking over a profitable business, they intend to take out a **salary** of £9,000 pa each. In their first year it will be slightly less as cash had to be injected in the first two months, compensated for in part by a drawing for a holiday in November.

If there are existing **staff** and you intend to keep them on, it is a simple matter to ask the vendor what they have been paid as a rough guide to your expenditure, bearing in mind minimum rates laid down by law.

Once you have paid the vendor for any prepaid **rates**, it would be wise to take advantage of the monthly payments systems offered. Usually business, domestic and water rates are payable over ten months, April to January inclusive.

The **repair and renewals** section should be looked upon as an allowance for maintenance and replacement of small items, *eg* brooms. It is *not* for replacing large pieces of equipment.

Bills for **gas** and **electricity** are normally presented quarterly. In the Brights' case, an extra £100 per month has been allowed in the summer to allow for heating the swimming pool. If no figures are available as a guide, advice can be obtained from the relevant company. You will no doubt also be told that, when running a business, commercial rates, which attract standard rate VAT, apply. If you are registered for VAT it is of little consequence as the tax can be claimed back, but if not, your costs can be a lot higher than you might have anticipated. In the current free market, competition between companies is fierce. Play one against the other and be ruthless in negotiating the best deal.

Advertising costs are very difficult to estimate, especially if you have nothing to guide you. Although the subject is dealt with in detail in Chapter 8, some books are devoted entirely to the subject and one lists 17 ways of arriving at an advertising budget!

Even the hotel in the most prominent position will rarely realise its full potential without some advertising, which includes brochures, and those off the beaten track will need more, certainly in the early stages. As a rough guide, allow between one and four per cent of estimated turnover, depending on your hotel's position. For our example we have shown the higher figure, spread over the year.

In running a small hotel, some form of **transport** is nearly always essential. It will rarely be possible for all supplies to be delivered, and certainly the best prices are obtainable only at a wholesale cash and carry.

An allowance may be claimed for occasions when your car is used *wholly* for your business. This may include, for example, collecting guests from the railway station, (providing your insurance company is agreeable). The Brights have decided to claim 50 per cent of their car running costs as a business expense and have included this figure on their cashflow chart.

Telephones, being part of the hotel equipment, are discussed in Chapter 6. The Brights have chosen to get a payphone installed for guests' use and will claim it as a business expense. Eighty per cent of the cost of the hotel private telephone will be claimed as business use. Bills are presented quarterly and include VAT.

Although it might be possible to delay paying the **professional fees** due until the following month, they have been included in the start-up costs. The same applies to membership of a **national trade association** and the local Hotels Association. The other figures are items of **equipment** they have decided to buy (see Chapter 6).

Since they have opted for a capital repayment 'holiday', only the **interest** on their £65,000 commercial mortgage is payable. The **setting-up charges**, which include the mortgage deed and associated legal costs, are payable when the loan is issued.

The **closing bank balance** each month becomes the opening one of the next month and reading along the bottom line shows what should be in the bank at any given time.

This forecast is most useful in concentrating the mind on how income is very quickly eroded by overheads. In cases where turnover is small as

RECEIPTS	JANUARY Budget Actual	FEBRUARY Budget Actual	MARCH Budget Actual	APRIL Budget Actual	MAY Budget Actual	JUNE Budget Actual	TOTALS Budget Actual
SALES (a)	425	850	5100	7235	8085	14470	36165
(Add Own Consumption)	300	300	300	300	300	300	1800
Less Provisions	830	665	950	1930	1650	3400	9425
GROSS PROFIT (b)	(105)	485	4450	5605	6735	11370	28540
Profit margin (b)/(a) x100							75.2%
OVERHEADS							
Salaries			2500	2250	2250	2250	9250
Rates	240	225	225	225	225	225	1365
Insurance	50	50	50	50	50	50	300
Repairs & renewals	70	60	60	60	60	60	370
Heat & Light	200	200	200	200	200	300	1300
Printing/postage/adverts	350	350	350	350	350	350	2100
Motor & Travel	80	80	80	80	80	80	480
Telephone	90	90	90	90	90	90	540
Prof. fees/licences	150	150	150	150	150	150	900
Bank interest	505	545	545	545	545	545	3230
M/ship fees/finance chgs	125	125	125	125	125	125	750
TOTAL OVERHEADS	1860	1875	4375	4125	4125	4225	20585
TRADING PROFIT							7955
Less depreciation	400	400	400	400	400	400	2400
NET PROFIT BEFORE TAX							5555

Fig. 9. Profit forecast for the Bourne Hotel, January to June.

RECEIPTS	JULY Budget Actual	AUGUST Budget Actual	SEPTEMBER Budget Actual	OCTOBER Budget Actual	NOVEMBER Budget Actual	DECEMBER Budget Actual	ANNUAL TOTAL Budget Actual
SALES (a)	14900	15320	13620	5100	425	5960	91490
(Add Own Consumption)	300	300	300	300	300	300	3600
Less Provisions	3350	3375	2910	1170	140	1350	21720
GROSS PROFIT (b)	11850	12245	11010	4230	585	4910	73370
Profit margin (b)/(a) x100							77.2%
OVERHEADS							
Salaries	2650	2650	2650	2250	4000	2000	25450
Rates	225	225	225	225	225	225	2715
Insurance	50	50	50	50	50	50	600
Repairs & renewals	60	60	60	60	60	60	730
Heat & Light	300	300	200	200	200	200	2700
Printing/postage/adverts	350	350	350	350	350	350	4200
Motor & Travel	80	80	80	80	80	80	960
Telephone	90	90	90	90	90	90	1080
Prof. fees/licences	150	150	150	150	150	150	1800
Bank interest	545	545	545	545	545	545	6500
M/ship fees/finance chgs	125	125	125	125	125	125	1500
TOTAL OVERHEADS	4625	4625	4525	4125	5875	3895	48235
TRADING PROFIT							25135
Less depreciation	400	400	400	400	400	400	4800
NET PROFIT BEFORE TAX							20335

Fig. 10. Profit forecast for the Bourne Hotel, July to December.

well as being seasonal, it is a very useful guide as to when and how much overdraft might be needed.

The profit forecast

Unlike the cashflow forecast, the profit forecast is designed to show you how profitable, or otherwise, the business is at the end of a given period, in this case a year. Some lenders may require a projection for two or more years to establish a hotel's long-term profitability.

Because it deals only with profit and loss, VAT is not an issue for those who are VAT-registered. For the Bourne, VAT has been deducted from all items which include the tax. Where, however, a hotel is not registered for VAT and takings are in consequence what are kept, VAT still has to be paid on some purchases and other items. In those circumstances, VAT, where applicable, will be included.

Although the seasonal element of the Bourne's turnover has been reflected in the profit forecast (Figures 9 and 10) most items can be averaged out over the twelve months. This includes the 'own consumption' figure which is an amount the tax inspector sets each year as an adjustment for board and lodging of the proprietors.

The figure shown is for two people and does not take account of tobacco, liquor, private use of car, 'exceptional repairs and replacements', or any expenditure of a personal nature. It will also vary according to the area and size of hotel. It is added to turnover as a non-monetary item.

Although your own drawings should be included, the tax inspector will add them back into the accounts when it comes to assessing profit.

As regards professional fees, you will remember the accountant said he was willing to defer his account until the year end in order to get your business. It is nevertheless an expense for the current year, along with what will be charged for handling your accounts, submitting them and negotiating with the Inland Revenue, and should be shown accordingly.

The only other item which may need some explanation at this stage is **depreciation**, dealt with in more detail in Chapter 7. Basically, it is an amount you deduct from the value of assets, *eg* equipment, to allow for the fact that it wears out.

As an example, if you estimate the life of a dishwasher to be ten years then, in broad terms, ten per cent of its original cost is deducted each year. If only five years, 20 per cent, and so on. Such capital items do not appear on your profit forecast but, of course, affect your cashflow and therefore appear on the cashflow forecast.

Much of the figure shown on our profit forecast is in respect of the car, typically reduced by 20 per cent pa on a reducing balance.

When complete, your business proposal should be typed, neat, tidy and well presented. A copy should be sent to the bank business manager a few days before you are due to see him. Since bankers tend to dress conservatively and you are embarking on a momentous step, you should be in the same condition as your business proposal (except typed). If done properly, your presentation will impress. It would be a pity if your appearance spoilt the overall impression.

Since no projections will ever work out exactly as planned, you may finally be asked for a **'break-even' figure**, so it will be as well to prepare one, just in case.

This is arrived at by multiplying your overheads (£48,235) by 100 then dividing by the gross profit margin, 77 per cent. In the example, a figure of £62,643 is produced, a reduction on the gross takings of £95,090 of some 34 per cent. A further reduction in turnover could be withstood if the Brights' drawings figures were reduced.

Do the same sort of exercise on your own projections. When you come to enter the actual figures, you will then know the percentage decrease in takings that can be tolerated while still leaving your business financially viable.

CHECKLIST

Have you:

- Sufficient funds available?
- Other sources of finance arranged?
- Assessed all possible sources?
- Obtained and studied the banks' business packs?
- Spoken to experts?
- Drawn up a start-up costs chart?
- Prepared a cashflow forecast?
- Prepared a profit forecast?
- Made a convincing business proposal?
- Worked out your break-even figure?
- Presented your proposals professionally?

5

Making Your Purchase

THE CONTRACT TO PURCHASE

Your solicitor will no doubt have advised you about the contract, particularly in respect of restrictive covenants. These need not be complicated but are designed to ensure you can operate your new business unhindered by anything the vendors may decide to do.

Debts

Since payment is normally made before a guest leaves, it is unusual to have any clients as debtors. The same may not be the case with your vendor since money might be owed to one or more suppliers. There may even be disputes outstanding on what is owed.

You will have enough problems of your own without getting involved in debts left by the vendor. It is up to your solicitor to ensure you are fully indemnified in this respect.

In the same vein, it is *not* a good idea to take over a vendor's VAT registration number since you would then be held responsible for any monies owing on that account (see Chapter 7 on VAT).

Restrictive covenants

A covenant should be included in the contract to protect your future trading position. Bearing in mind what has been said about guests following individuals, would you want to see your vendor set up shop in another hotel just up the road?

Contracts should include terms as favourable to you as your solicitor can secure. Though the vendor, at this juncture, might genuinely have not the slightest intention of staying in the hotel business, circumstances change and intentions with them.

If your solicitor can get agreement to a covenant that restricts the vendor from trading within a 25-mile radius for the next ten years, great. If not, a watering-down might be necessary. But don't give in and agree to terms you think are inadequate.

Assess the type of hotel you are buying in terms of how much trade is repeat business. If much of it is, stick out for a covenant that will ensure you a clear run until you get established — irrespective of what the vendor might say.

Make sure you know where the vendor is going once the hotel has been vacated. The fact that a contract has been agreed to and signed does not, of course, mean the vendor is physically unable to break any of the terms; it merely means you can seek redress in law. In case this course should prove necessary, it is important that the terms entered in a contract are seen to be reasonable. Those deemed unreasonable are unlikely to be upheld by a court.

Other clauses

Circumstances peculiar to your hotel may indicate that other clauses should be included. For example, the vendor should continue to trade and/or take bookings on your behalf up to the date of completion.

Further clauses will, of course, be necessary if the property is leasehold. The need for a very experienced solicitor to negotiate the right terms for you in a lease agreement cannot be over-emphasised.

INSURANCE

In a nutshell, insurance can be divided into two categories:

- that which is optional, *eg* to cover disasters and other risks
- that which is required by law, *eg* motor insurance.

In the hotel business, under the **Employers Liability (Compulsory Insurance) Act 1969** it is compulsory to provide employers' liability insurance, and if you are leasing equipment the leasing company may oblige you to insure it as part of the contract. Further, if you are buying the hotel with a loan, the lenders will require their investment to be insured.

Although, otherwise, insurance might not be compulsory, it is highly recommended in order to keep you solvent if disaster should strike. And strike it does! Slates fly off roofs in very high winds; a guest with typhoid fever can cause your hotel to be closed down for a while; thieving is commonplace, maybe even by your staff.

What to insure against

There are a number of risks that apply peculiarly to hotels, leading several insurance companies to issue policies specially for people like you.

The best and most comprehensive policy you can afford (without paying for risks that don't apply to your hotel) should be the one to go for. Whatever the cost, it will be but a fraction of the claim if, for example,

The Building	The Contents	Glass Breakage	Consequential Loss	Loss of Money	Liabilities	
					To Staff	To Public
Take out cover against all usual risks on exchange of contract	Strongly advised	Highly advisable especially with children	Advisable to protect profits	Advisable to protect takings before bank takes responsibility	Mandatory	Highly advisable
	Own contents to be insured separately				Exhibit Certificate	Exhibit Notice
Continued cover highly advisable	Consider seasonal stock increases			Consider Fidelity Insurance		Consider additional sums
Consider accidental damage cover	Consider accidental damage cover					Add product liability?

Think about additional cover: *eg* Personal Accident, Frozen Food, Computer Breakdown, Legal Expenses, Goods in Transit, Loss of Liquor Licence, Failure of Services.

- Discuss fully with knowledgeable insurance broker.
- Obtain competitive quotations. Check/compare excesses.
- Local package available?
- Pay premium monthly if interest rate reasonable.

Fig. 11. Considering insurance.

one of your guests should leave a lighted cigarette end in an armchair and your hotel, or even part of it, was gutted by fire.

Your friendly, knowledgeable insurance broker will be able to give specific advice and, particularly in a resort, a package deal may have been negotiated with an insurance company leading to very cost-effective terms being offered.

The following is typical of the sort of cover offered in hotel policies:

● **Buildings:** covering all the usual risks associated with domestic policies. Accidental damage cover may be added.

● **Contents:** to include stock, business furniture, computer systems, records and so on against most risks (which may include leakage of beer). Seasonal peak stock increases to suit *your* hotel can be allowed for. Accidental damage cover, sometimes an optional extra, should be taken out, particularly if young children are accepted.

● **Business interruption**: covers loss of profits due to incidents beyond your control, *eg* a gas leak at nearby premises preventing access to yours, outbreak of infectious disease, poisoning by food or drink you provided. At least one policy includes oil pollution of the nearby coastline.

● **Loss of money**: money which is on the premises, in transit or in a bank night safe. Various limits apply according to where the money was, *eg* in a safe, and in what form it was, *eg* cheques, and when it was stolen. Fraud or dishonesty of an employee, known as fidelity insurance, may be covered under this section.

● **Glass**: fixed interior and exterior, display units, counter cases, shelves, signs and mirrors are covered.

● **Liabilities**: to employees for bodily injury, illness or disease arising out of and in the course of their employment (the certificate showing you are covered for this liability must be clearly displayed in your hotel); to guests and members of the public for bodily injury, illness or disease plus loss of or damage to their property which arises in connection with your business, including your liability from the consumption of food and drink.

It must be said that liability to *resident* guests for loss or damage to property is a grey area, due in no small part to **The Hotel Proprietors**

Act 1956. (In Northern Ireland **The Hotel Proprietors (Northern Ireland) Act 1958.**)

Covered by the Act are 'establishments held out by the proprietor as offering food, drink and, if so required, sleeping accommodation without special contract, to any traveller presenting himself who appears able and willing to pay a reasonable sum for the services and facilities provided and who is in a fit state to be received.'

Does this Act apply to your hotel? If so, and it is difficult to see which hotels can claim to be exempt, a notice must be displayed (Figure 12, also Chapter 9) which limits a hotelier's liability to £50 for any one article and a maximum of £100 per guest (unless property has been deposited, or offered for deposit for safe keeping) and does not cover vehicles of any kind or property left in them.

The display of such a notice will be a condition of the hotel insurance and will so limit the company's liability to the sums mentioned. Although guests will often have cover under their own domestic policies, additional cover beyond the sums mentioned in the Act may be taken out at extra cost.

A range of cover beyond the basics is offered to enable insurance to be tailored to a hotelier's particular requirements. Such cover may include:

- **Personal accident**: cash compensation and/or income for principals and employees.

- **Frozen food**: in the event of breakdown of appliances or accidental failure of the electricity supply.

- **Small computers**: loss, damage or breakdown of equipment and/or data.

- **Legal expenses**: disputes, including those with employees and customers, and other legal costs.

- **Goods in transit**: being carried, loaded or unloaded.

- **Book debts**: where books which are the only record of debts are destroyed.

- **Loss of licence**: if your liquor licence is lost or not renewed through causes beyond your control.

NOTICE

LOSS OF OR DAMAGE TO GUESTS' PROPERTY

Under the Hotel Proprietors Act 1956, a hotel proprietor may in certain circumstances be liable to make good any loss of or damage to a guest's property even though it was not due to any fault of the proprietor or staff of the hotel.

This liability however–

(a) extends only to the property of guests who have engaged sleeping accommodation at the hotel;

(b) is limited to £50 for any one article and a total of £100 in the case of any one guest, except in the case of property which has been deposited, or offered for deposit, for safe custody;

(c) does not cover motor cars or other vehicles of any kind or any property left in them or horses or other live animals.

This notice does not constitute an admission either that the Act applies to this hotel or that liability thereunder attaches to the proprietor of this hotel in any particular case.

Fig. 12. Notice of loss or damage.

- **Failure of vital services**: breakdown in electricity, gas or water supplies.

- **Key man insurance**: to compensate for the loss of a vital member of staff.

It should be noted that the contents of your private accommodation are not insured under a hotel policy (but may be under a Guest House policy) and *must* be insured separately.

Where to get insurance
It is as well to obtain prospectuses from various companies, to check through them and pick out the sort of cover which suits you best. Your local insurance broker will help you with some and other companies may be approached direct. The **British Hospitality Association** also has special schemes for members.

Occasionally you will have no choice since some lenders advance loans with insurance built in. You will often pay much more than you need under such arrangements, which are best avoided.

What to watch out for

- What you may consider to be unreasonable excesses (the amount companies deduct from claim payments).

- The facility to pay premiums monthly without the imposition of an excessive interest rate — it will help your cashflow.

- Your obligation to insure the structure of your new hotel as soon as contracts have been exchanged. Many companies will add a small amount to the annual premium for the period of time, usually a few weeks, they were on risk for the buildings part of the insurance.

If you should insure your hotel for a sum which is less than its full rebuilding cost, 'average' will apply to *all* claims — for example, 20 per cent undervalued, 20 per cent deducted from *every* claim.

MOVING IN — WHAT DO WE NEED TO DO?

Taking over the guests

You will already have found out how expensive advertising is. Do you want to continue paying out these large, ever-increasing sums? No one in their right mind will want to erode the profits by advertising more than is necessary.

The cheapest and best form of advertising is your guests. You will want them to sing your praises. To do that, they will need to be impressed.

If guests are in residence when you move in, a few minutes spent with the vendor (faithful notebook and pen in hand) finding out whether they have been before, how long they intend to stay and what their special preferences, dislikes and foibles are, can pay handsome dividends. 'But I don't have the set menu. I'm a vegetarian,' as you are serving dinner will impress no one, especially the cook!

Try to convince any guests in residence that you can do just as good a job as the vendor and that they should transfer their loyalty to you. If you happen to upstage the vendor, without overdoing it, all well and good.

Taking over the bookings

You will find any deposits taken in respect of future bookings included in a reconciliation statement prepared by your solicitor to accompany the contract.

Before the vendor disappears, you should know more about those who have booked. Have they been before? Do they know the vendor will not be there when they arrive? Have they previously stated any preferences, *e.g.* not eating fish?

Now is the time to start building up information on all your guests so you can refer to your records when they phone up or just before they arrive. Unless you have a photographic memory, an A4-size index book will do nicely. Without letting them know how you remember things like whether they take cream in coffee, they will be impressed. Everyone likes to be treated as someone special. Impressing them without being sycophantic should be your aim.

A word of warning! Should you enter personal details, some of which may not be complimentary, on a computer, under the **Data Protection Act 1998** guests can demand a copy of information you hold about them. You may also need to notify the Data Protection Commissioner, Wycliffe House, Water Lane, Wilmslow, Cheshire SK9 5AF, Tel: (01625) 545745, and pay an annual fee (in 2000, £35). If you keep only sufficient data as is necessary for your records, accounts and staff administration, it is unlikely you will need to notify but, to make sure, send for a self-assessment guide. All other aspects of the Act still apply. Manual records are covered as well (there is no need to notify) and from October 2001, unless you are temporarily exempt under transitional arrangements, staff as well as guests will have the right to access most of what is written about them. Watch what you write! Since CCTV data is also covered by the Act, should you have such a system, enquire as to how the law might affect you.

Taking over the stock

Stocktakers are specialist individuals who, traditionally, list and evaluate stock at the beginning or end of a trading period or when a business changes hands. Unless a hotel is large with extensive stock, it will rarely be worth paying fees to a stocktaker.

A small hotel will most likely, as a maximum, have a few hundred pounds' worth of stock in the close season and if you check it yourself you will know exactly what you are getting and can choose what to take and what to leave.

Firstly, remember you must never pay more than the vendor paid for it and, if VAT-registered, the tax will already have been accounted for on the return to the Customs and Excise and must not be paid again by you. Indeed, nothing you take over when buying a business should attract VAT.

Check all stock against invoices and you will then see how old it is. Some vendors are dishonest, no matter how they may have appeared when you met them, and the last thing you want to do is to pay for stock which is past its sell-by-date. It may be that a crate of out-of-date fruit juices has been slipped in at the bottom of the pile.

Allow sufficient time on the morning you are taking over to check thoroughly and tick off what stock you are prepared to pay for. If you find there has been an attempt to fob you off with old stock, become ruthless.

Taking over the inventory

In the same way that your surveyor will have checked over the fabric of the hotel, so you must be just as thorough in checking the inventory (the list of fixtures, fittings, furniture and equipment that goes with the hotel). You will already have started when you listed the kitchen equipment on your first or second visit to the hotel. Now is the time to ensure that an old refrigerator hasn't been left in the place of the new one you saw when you were making notes!

Before moving in, so that any justified price reduction could be negotiated, you should have checked over items like crockery and cutlery to ensure you have enough that match. If replacements have become unobtainable, you may need to change the lot.

As mentioned in Chapter 2, all items of furniture need careful checking to ensure they haven't worn out and that they satisfy the new fire safety regulations. It may already have been acknowledged by the vendor that you will need to replace furniture and the fact reflected in the asking price. If not, replacement of substantial amounts of furniture that might soon be illegal for you to use could erode your profits for years to come.

Report any disputed items to your solicitor straight away so that adjustments, after due negotiation, can be made.

Taking over the liquor licence

If taking over a licensed hotel, completion day will normally have been scheduled to coincide with a sitting of the Licensing Justices so that you can get immediate protection of the law to sell intoxicating liquor.

The police will already have made their enquiries about you to see if you can be considered a fit person to hold a licence, and you will have been made aware if any objection is to be raised.

It is normal for there to be a clause in the contract that releases you from your obligation to purchase if the protection of a licence is not transferred to you. This eventuality is almost unheard of without prior notice. However, having attended the Court hearing, usually with your solicitor and the outgoing licensee, it is not until you hear the magistrate tell you a protection order has been granted that you can call yourself a hotelier.

Points to consider

There are a number of bodies you should inform when you begin working for yourself:

● The Inland Revenue about your self-employed status. The legal obligation is to give notification within six months of the end of the year of assessment in which you started your business. You may otherwise incur interest on unpaid tax and penalties.

● The Contributions Agency (now merged with the Inland Revenue) with the object of registering for self-employed National Insurance contributions (see Chapter 7).

● The Customs & Excise VAT office if you are to be VAT registered (see Chapter 7).

● The Environmental Health Department of the local authority to register your premises under the Food Safety Act (see Chapter 3).

● The Rating Department of the local authority.

● The suppliers of the public utilities used.

● The Inland Revenue PAYE section if you are to employ staff.

● The Data Protection Commissioner if you are to keep records of guests on a computer.

MAKING CHANGES

There are probably a dozen things you are itching to put right the moment you move in. Try to resist the temptation. Hasty changes made on day one might be regretted later and could prove costly.

Should we change the hotel name?

If you are taking over a going concern, think *very* carefully before you change the name of your hotel. Whatever its name, it is the one by which a lot of people know it, including the local **Tourist Information Centre** staff and all the previous guests. It is also the name that appears in telephone directories and probably in a number of guide books. The latter, in particular, can circulate for several years before new editions are bought.

You may, of course, intend to change the whole way in which the business is run, maybe upgrade it and push up the prices, virtually starting again from scratch. Or it may not have been a hotel before, in which case the choice is yours — within reason.

It is obvious you will neither be able nor want to name your hotel after another in the area. In addition, no matter how grand you want the name to sound, there are certain words and expressions you are prohibited from using without the express permission of the Secretary of State for Trade and Industry. International, British, Royal, King, Prince and Duke are but a few. The use of some words even constitutes a criminal offence.

Also avoid gimmicky or clever names. If you try to be clever and choose The Pits or Fawlty Towers you may find your hotel difficult or impossible to sell on in the future.

When choosing a name, think long and hard about the image you want to portray in the minds of the type of people you expect to be reading about your hotel. It needs to create an attraction (see page 142 on advertising).

Should your hotel be leasehold, you will need the owner's permission to change the name.

Stationery

Is printed stationery the sort of thing you would expect someone running your type of hotel to have? If so, choose that which goes with your hotel and colour co-ordinate everything.

If you consider it right for you to project a highly professional image, apart from letterheads, brochures, invoices and tariff sheets, you may wish to consider having printed booking confirmations (discussed in Chapter 9) setting out the deposit paid, terms for payment of the balance and guests' obligations in law. Using NCR paper would be sensible as it provides you with a copy; you would need to make sure it could be supplied to match your chosen colour scheme.

Much thought should be given before ordering stationery. Under **The Business Names Act 1985** any business not disclosing in its title the name/s of the owner/s or partner/s must show such information, together with an address at which documents could be served, on all:

- business letters
- written orders for the supply of goods or services
- invoices and receipts issued in the course of the business
- written demands for payment of debts arising in the course of the business.

It is also a requirement of the Act that a notice setting out the same information should be prominently displayed in the hotel. A typical notice is shown in Figure 13. (See also Chapter 9).

PARTICULARS OF OWNERSHIP
OF

The Bourne Hotel

as required by section 4 of the Business Names Act 1985

Full Names of Owners   *Address within Great Britain at which documents relating to the business may be effectively served*

Andrew Alan BRIGHT   196 The Esplanade, Surfbourne
Christine BRIGHT   Surfshire, SF91 5QT

Fig. 13. Notice of ownership.

Leaflets setting out the provisions of the Act are available free of charge from:

Companies House
Crown Way
Cardiff CF4 3UZ
Tel: (029) 2038 0801.
Fax: (029) 2038 0517.
Email: emailenquiries@companieshouse.gov.uk

Enquiries in Scotland should be addressed to:

The Registrar of Companies for Scotland
Companies House
37 Castle Terrace
Edinburgh EH1 2EB

Tel: (0131) 535 5800.
Fax: (0131) 535 5820.
Web: www.companieshouse.gov.uk

In choosing stationery, and particularly brochures (discussed further in Chapter 8), ask yourself how you want to project your business. Remember your aim should be to impress your customers, which means neither under- nor over-impressing. A posh brochure full of colour photographs would be very much of an overkill for a small B and B (and could well use up a year's profits!). In such a situation you might consider printed stationery is an expense you could do without, though business cards are always useful. Think carefully, spend wisely. If you have a computer, the necessary software, the know-how and, of course, the time, you can produce all your own stationery quite cheaply. You could even produce your own brochures with those impressive colour photos!

VAT registration numbers, if appropriate, need to be shown on all invoices together with other VAT-related information (see Chapter 7).

Other changes

Acting hastily without taking expert advice or time to think things through can prove costly. It is no good installing another radiator if it transpires the boiler is already working over capacity. Worse still, you could buy a new piece of expensive catering equipment only to realise it doesn't comply with the provisions of the Food Safety Act.

By all means chuck out that hideous picture on the reception area wall; more important decisions need deeper thought.

CHECKLIST

Have you:

- Ensured the contract to purchase meets with your approval?
- Arranged adequate insurance?
- Timed your move correctly?
- Made contact with your local Hotels Association?
- Obtained list/special requirements of guests?
- Obtained full details of bookings?
- Carefully checked the stock and inventory?
- Reconciled all monies re existing guests' bills, deposits on bookings, stock and inventory?
- Carefully considered any changes you intend to make?

6

Assessing Equipment and Staffing

Equipment and the level of staffing are to some extent linked. The more efficient your equipment, the less staff you are likely to need. Since staff can create problems as well as reduce your profits, you will benefit by carefully assessing your equipment needs.

ASSESSING AND BUYING EQUIPMENT

You will already have made an initial assessment of the hotel equipment and taken it into account when agreeing a final price. It is now time for a detailed assessment.

The kitchen

The kitchen is, without doubt, the engine room of your hotel. If guests' food is not right you will not get them back, and if the kitchen is inadequately equipped you will have a job to get the food right. At the least, it will make life far more difficult for the cook and/or the kitchen staff than it need be.

Keep things in perspective, though. If you are running a small B and B with only two letting bedrooms, you should be able to cater for your guests as if they were part of the family, with little or no commercial catering equipment. (You still need to comply with the food hygiene regulations — see page 43).

As premises get larger, and particularly if you provide evening meals, catering for guests requires a far more professional approach. The secret is to have *precisely* what you need.

- Have individual items the right size for your needs, neither too large nor too small.
- Have the right amount of equipment, neither any items you will never use nor too few to make for efficiency.

It is surprising how many hotel kitchens catering for, say, ten or more guests, contain not one single item of commercial equipment. Yet it can make life so much easier and the whole catering operation much more efficient. Such equipment, which comes in a variety of sizes, is generally much more robust than its domestic equivalent, more powerful but, you've guessed it, more expensive.

Take a look at what might suit you in a small hotel kitchen:

- **Cookers.** Some will consider it essential to have the right capacity cooker, capable of producing the variety of food you intend to serve. Once the right cooker is installed, the rest of your kitchen can be built around it. Ranges are designed to slot together. Remarkably sophisticated combination cookers are on the market, some with probes to continuously monitor the inside temperature of the food.

- **Hotplates.** Often separate from the cooker and so can use different fuels for convenience. Four will rarely be enough.

- **Microwave ovens.** Far more powerful and robust than domestic versions, therefore faster and more versatile. Booklets to help you make the most of your professional microwave oven are available free from some manufacturers.

- **Fryers.** Can be free-standing, built-in or mobile. If chips are a regular feature of your menu, if only for children, the right fryer can be invaluable.

- **Griddles.** Very useful for beefburgers, steaks, chops and for breakfasts.

- **Grills.** Can be wall-mounted, free-standing or built-in. Combination grills/griddles are available.

- **Bains Marie.** For hot storage of soups and vegetables.

- **Toasters.** Various models have a capacity of between 60 and 380 slices an hour, and keep it hot after toasting.

- **Dishwashers.** For highly efficient cleaning of crockery, cutlery and sometimes pans. Washing cycles range from two minutes to about half an hour.

- **Hot water boilers.** Can be likened to a constant kettle. Virtually essential when producing numerous pots of tea and coffee.

- **Hot cupboards.** Useful for preheating plates and for keeping food hot prior to serving. Note that a minimum temperature of 63°C is laid down under The Food Safety Act when keeping food hot.

- **Refrigerators and freezers.** In a busy kitchen, only commercial models can cope with the demands laid down by The Food Safety Act. Certain foodstuffs need to be kept at temperatures no higher than 5°C. For maximum efficiency, self-defrosting models should be used. Some have fan-assistance for quick chilling.

- **Miscellaneous.** Worksurfaces, shelving, cookerhoods, coffee machines, utensils and knives. Domestic quality pans will usually wear out very quickly if used heavily.

Since high standards of hygiene are essential and all surfaces need to be smooth, impervious, durable and easy to clean, it is normal for commercial catering equipment to be produced in stainless steel.

Reputable catering equipment companies will be only too pleased to advise you on the items best suited to your kitchen and may design a layout free of charge providing you purchase equipment from them. Such companies may submit layouts to the local Environmental Health Department for approval before installation.

In addition to the actual catering equipment, under your Fire Certificate you will be required to provide a fire blanket, preferably near your kitchen exit door.

An actual small hotel kitchen layout is shown in Figure 14.

As with most, it is not perfect. Always consider the distances between key points:

- where the goods are unloaded
- where they are stored
- where food preparation takes place
- where the food is rested prior to cooking
- where the food is cooked
- where it is rested after cooking
- where it is assembled for serving
- where it is held prior to serving.

It can thus be worked out how much walking is required during the whole operation. It should obviously be kept to a minimum within the constraints imposed by individual hotel layouts.

Note the necessity for a separate basin for hand-washing, also the advisability of separate preparation areas to reduce the possibility of food cross-contamination.

Consideration should always be given to the electrical supply. Some equipment requires more than a 13 amp socket and a number of demands can cause the system to be overloaded. Advice should be sought from either the electricity company or a competent electrician.

Under the **Provisions and Use of Work Equipment Regulations 1998** you have a duty to consider the suitability, use (including training of employees), hazards, maintenance and safety of all equipment used.

Further, the **Gas Safety (Installation and Use) Regulations 1998** and the **Electrical Equipment (Safety) Regulations 1994**, together with various other sets of related regulations, need to be complied with. These regulations, as amended, also cover the safety, maintenance and use of all relevant equipment and appliances throughout your establishment. Consult your local **Environmental Health Officer** or **Trading Standards** department for the latest requirements. Call the Health & Safety Executive advice line (0800 300363) for information about gas safety matters.

Laundry

You will be wise to make arrangements for guests' laundry. If you don't, particularly where small children are involved, items, some of them not very savoury, will be washed in the sink or bath and draped over radiators, heaters and the like. Considerable damage can be caused to decorations.

Some hoteliers can tell stories about socks and intimate items of underwear being boiled in kettles supplied to rooms for teamaking. Are you now convinced you need to make some arrangements?

These can vary between offering a complete, efficient laundry service with 'next day' returns and making a washing machine and tumble dryer, suitably sited in a separate room, available for guests' own use. If providing a laundry room, domestic appliances will soon fail under heavy use and consideration should be given to using commercial equipment.

It may be onerous to wash and dry guests' laundry yourself but it is infinitely preferable to offering nothing.

The public rooms

After the outside, public rooms are what give people their initial impression of your hotel. Whatever the image you want to project, your success or failure will be influenced by what guests think as soon as they set foot inside the door.

Were you impressed when you first stepped inside? If not, what was wrong? It is important to set about making it as welcoming as you would have liked to see it. First impressions can last.

Everywhere should look warm and comfortable, tidy, uncluttered and relaxing. Soft though adequate lighting, if possible on walls, will help. Central hanging white lights give an impression of starkness.

You are now well aware of the fire safety regulations. If they mean you will have to change or reupholster any furniture, choose replacements with care. It's no good paying for a very expensive three-piece suite if the next week someone's unruly offspring are likely to be jumping all over it and wiping their greasy hands on it. Many kids are well behaved — some aren't! Select your furniture to suit the type of hotel you are running.

The dining room

The dining room should also be welcoming, preferably with wall lights, soft but sufficient for the guests to see what they're eating. It's no good serving fantastic food if they can't see it, or the surroundings let you down.

If you need to replace dining room tables, choose square ones which will each accommodate two people yet can be pushed together for larger groups. Polished wood with place mats looks good but is not advised if you take young children.

If you are planning a dining room from scratch and you don't want to use small tables, a square one to seat four should measure at least 900mm and a rectangular one for six 1500mm by 900mm. About a 700mm space is needed for drawing back a chair to get in and out, more if it's necessary for others to walk past. Room should be left, if possible, for somewhere to put cereals, fruit juice, cutlery and perhaps a coffee machine.

Music

Guests talk in a more relaxed manner if there is subtle music in the background. Dining rooms can otherwise resemble a morgue, with guests either whispering or seemingly afraid to speak.

Even many seasoned hoteliers are unaware of the fact that, under the **Copyright, Design and Patents Act 1988**, if music is played in public, which means anywhere outside your domestic circle, licences may be required. Music live, on radio, television or by sound recording is included in the regulations.

In other words, if you provide for your guests any music at all that you haven't composed yourself, you may need a licence from:

The *Performing Right Society*
Elwes House
19 Church Walk
Peterborough PE1 2UZ.

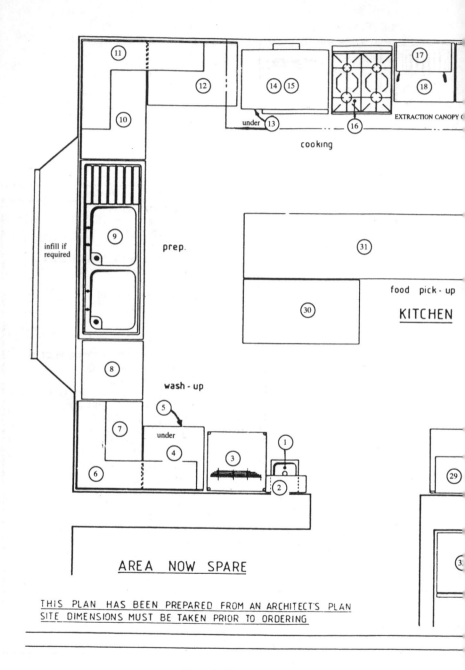

Fig. 14. Kitchen plan.

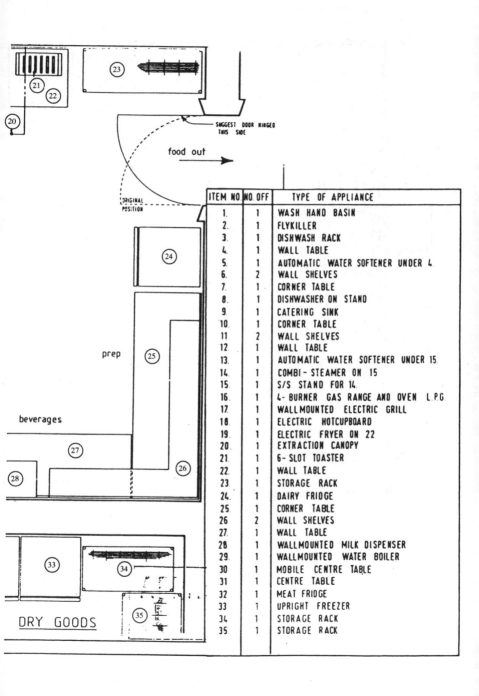

SUGGEST DOOR HINGED
THIS SIDE

food out →

ORIGINAL
POSITION

prep

beverages

DRY GOODS

ITEM NO.	NO. OFF	TYPE OF APPLIANCE
1.	1	WASH HAND BASIN
2.	1	FLYKILLER
3.	1	DISHWASH RACK
4.	1	WALL TABLE
5.	1	AUTOMATIC WATER SOFTENER UNDER 4.
6.	2	WALL SHELVES
7.	1	CORNER TABLE
8.	1	DISHWASHER ON STAND
9.	1	CATERING SINK
10.	1	CORNER TABLE
11	2	WALL SHELVES
12	1	WALL TABLE
13.	1	AUTOMATIC WATER SOFTENER UNDER 15.
14.	1	COMBI - STEAMER ON 15
15.	1	S/S STAND FOR 14.
16.	1	4- BURNER GAS RANGE AND OVEN L.P.G.
17.	1	WALLMOUNTED ELECTRIC GRILL
18.	1	ELECTRIC HOTCUPBOARD
19.	1	ELECTRIC FRYER ON 22
20.	1	EXTRACTION CANOPY
21.	1	6- SLOT TOASTER
22.	1	WALL TABLE
23.	1	STORAGE RACK
24.	1	DAIRY FRIDGE
25.	1	CORNER TABLE
26	2	WALL SHELVES
27.	1	WALL TABLE
28	1	WALLMOUNTED MILK DISPENSER
29.	1	WALLMOUNTED WATER BOILER
30	1	MOBILE CENTRE TABLE
31	1	CENTRE TABLE
32	1	MEAT FRIDGE
33	1	UPRIGHT FREEZER
34.	1	STORAGE RACK
35.	1	STORAGE RACK

Tel: 0800 0684828.

Fax: (01733) 312912

Web: www.prs.co.uk

Further, if you play recorded music for your guests as background music, an additional licence may be needed from the body to whom record companies have assigned their copyright:

Phonographic Performance Ltd

1 Upper James Street

London W1R 3HG

Tel: (020) 7534 1000.

Fax: (020) 75341111.

Web: www.ppluk.com

Tariffs vary greatly according to the situation but, as a rough guide, for a small hotel with up to 15 bedrooms and which does not admit the general public, expect to pay about £85 to PRS (plus 50 per cent if caught illegally without a license by an inspector) and about the same to PPL. All rates are plus VAT.

The bar

A bar can be very costly to set up. Apart from the bar itself, a good selection of glasses is needed and shelving to put them on, optics, measures, ice buckets, stools and a host of bits and pieces like bottle openers, a board for lemons, oranges, and so on. When taking over a bar, make sure you are left a reasonable number of glasses and ancillary equipment.

Should you intend to buy new optics, under the **Weights and Measures (Intoxicating Liquor) Order 1988**, as amended, only measures of 25ml, or multiples thereof, are legal.

If your bar is not conducive to guests relaxing after a (hopefully) good meal, they will go elsewhere. As a result, you will be tied to hanging around just in case someone wants serving, your perishable stock will deteriorate and, instead of making a handsome profit, your bar could run at a loss.

Take prompt steps to ensure your bar projects the right image — soft lighting, sweet background music. In other words, create the right atmosphere for your guests to spend money.

Incidentally, the Fire Authority needs to know about any new bar or alteration in the location of an existing one. Running a bar is also discussed in Chapters 2 and 9.

The bedrooms

If guests are unable to sleep because of uncomfortable beds, they will stay only as long as they have to, will not come back and will not speak about your hotel favourably to their friends. It is as simple as that.

Far too few hoteliers pay sufficient attention to the condition of their guests' beds. You can gain an immediate advantage over your competitors by providing firm, comfortable beds that don't squeak, or worse, clang. This is particularly important if you have a honeymoon suite. It's funny for everyone else, but not for the couple concerned.

The **English Tourism Council** lays down a minimum standard for all serviced accommodation and publishes a booklet, available to the general public, listing the various standards. Potential guests can therefore ascertain the standard of facilities they can expect.

The *Standards Leaflet* is obtainable from the English Tourism Council, Tel: (020) 8563 3000, and from Regional Tourist Boards. It also contains a list of standards required for disabled people. These 'harmonised standards', agreed by the Tourist Boards, the AA and the RAC, replacing the crown grading system with one using diamonds, are shown in the Appendix. Larger hotels retain star gradings.

Fees are charged for annual inspections and membership (which has fringe benefits) according to the size of hotel.

As with other furniture, beds and pillows may need to comply with fire safety regulations.

The public's expectation of standards in hotels is continually rising, due in no small part to en suite bathrooms being provided on most holidays abroad. It is an increasing trend for guests not to make a booking unless they can be assured of a bathroom, including a wc, en suite to their bedroom (see page 30).

Guests often like to relax in their bedrooms other than at night-time. Aim to provide two easy chairs in each double bedroom if at all possible.

A few companies specialise in equipment for hotel bedrooms. Amongst the items offered are:

- Television sets. With or without satellite facility. Excellent for most guests, purgatory if the walls are thin and their neighbours like late-night viewing, especially if the viewers are hard of hearing! Current concessions allow for up to 15 sets to be operated in hotels for one broadcasting licence fee. Above that number, one licence for every five sets.

- Tea/coffee trays. These enable guests to make beverages whenever they want. Virtually eliminates the need for tea/coffee room service.

- Hairdryers. Women often want to wash their hair while away from home. A nice facility if you can afford it.

- Trouser presses. A real boon for the men, especially after a long journey.

- Luggage racks. Keep dusty cases off your bed covers.

In mostly larger hotels, room equipment is often further enhanced by the provision of minibars, safes and even video recorders. Telephones are dealt with below. Companies leasing hotel bedroom equipment offer package deals to tempt you to provide a greater range of facilities.

As explained in Chapter 3, notices in a set format must be displayed to tell guests what to do if fire breaks out.

General
Outside the kitchen and bedrooms, there is other equipment essential to the smooth and efficient running of a hotel.

Telephones
Guests, whether on holiday or business, will always want the use of a telephone. In up-market situations a direct-dial system can be installed in each bedroom with an appropriate number of lines. In more modest establishments, the cost of such a system couldn't be justified. Yet you don't want your own line kept busy with guests chatting about the weather while others are trying unsuccessfully to make a booking. Not all your guests will have a mobile, so the answer is a payphone exclusively for guests' use. With high usage, it is possible to recoup the rental since you empty the moneybox yourself and calls are charged at double what they cost you.

Cleaners
Large quantities of grime and grit are regularly walked into hotel floor coverings. This means that domestic quality carpets will not stand the wear and tear for long and a powerful cleaner is a necessity. Domestic vacuum cleaners are not made for such heavy use and, if not already on the inventory, consideration should be given to a heavy duty commercial one.

Computers
Computers are rarely feasible as a business tool in very small establishments but, for those a little larger, should be considered. Ensure you can get the sort of program you require before committing yourself. To get one just right could prove costly. Applications available include stationery, brochures, (both with big savings over conventional printers), spreadsheets for accounts, etc, and even advertising on the Internet. If

you advertise in your Local Authority tourist guide, your hotel could be included on their web site. The benefits that are derived from having a web page (or pages) varies from hotel to hotel. It will rarely be viable to go to the expense of paying for the creation of your own, but you can set one up yourself (see *Creating a Web Site* in this series). If you have a web site it is vitally important that it contains sufficient information and that all data, particularly if you publish tariffs or make special offers, is updated regularly. If you are using a PC for accounts, speak to your accountant since the Inland Revenue and, if VAT-registered, the Customs and Excise, need to be able to access the data.

Heating

An efficient heating system you can switch on at a moment's notice to cope with our changeable climate, and capable of providing sufficient hot water for nearly all your guests to bath or shower at virtually the same time, is absolutely essential. Free-standing heating appliances can easily be knocked over and are usually a contravention of the requirements of the Fire Certificate. If there is any intention to use portable heating appliances, the advice of your local Fire Safety Advisor should be sought.

Fire equipment and lighting

Fire extinguishers need to be provided where a Fire Certificate is either necessary or in force. Various fire extinguishing agents suit the different types of fire, *eg* those involving gases or electrical equipment. Before purchasing any fire extinguisher, seek the advice of your Fire Safety Advisor, no matter what any salesperson might say. As a condition of each Fire Certificate, emergency lighting must be provided to illuminate all escape routes and to enable fire alarm call points and firefighting equipment to be located. Again, seek the expert advice of your Fire Safety Advisor.

To purchase or lease equipment?

The advantage of buying outright, whether by means of a loan or otherwise, is that you own the asset, so enhancing your balance sheet and enabling you to claim a capital allowance (see page 122). The main disadvantage is that it can use up large amounts of cash which you may need to borrow.

A further disadvantage of purchasing equipment is that in fields which are changing rapidly, *eg* computers, your asset can quickly be out of date and therefore worthless. No one wants an obsolete piece of equipment.

Try to work out the lifespan of each item you want and the effect improved technology may have upon it. If in doubt, it is better to go for a leasing agreement. Try to get one with an option to renew or purchase at the end of an agreed minimum period. Get a second opinion from your accountant.

The exterior

Lighting of the right shade and intensity will enhance the look of your hotel and make people want to venture inside. Remember your all-important aim to impress. The extra on your electricity bill can pale into insignificance beside the increased business.

You may consider it beneficial to have a big, illuminated sign outside. If so, do bear in mind that signs and the lighting for them are subject to planning law. Consult a Planning Officer before splashing out.

A sign you *must* have, either outside or in the reception area, is one that shows your prices (unless your hotel is very small).

The Tourism (Sleeping Accommodation Price Display) Order 1977 provides that hotels which offer accommodation to guests who have not booked in advance, and which have at least four bedrooms or eight beds, must display a legible notice in a prominent position at the entrance or in the reception area, to include:

- the price of a bedroom for one person
- the price of a bedroom for two persons
- the price of a bed in any other type of bedroom
- if the prices include VAT, this must be stated
- if there is a service charge it must be included
- if meals are included in the accommodation charge this must be stated
- any additional information providing it does not detract from the prominence of the required information.

You could have different notices reflecting, as appropriate, the variation in charges according to the season. A typical such notice is shown in Figure 15.

In displaying a notice, it must be borne in mind that to mislead a customer as to the price charged is an offence under **The Consumer Protection Act 1987**, Section 20. A further offence is committed if you fail to inform a customer if you raise a price after quoting it (excluding changes in VAT).

The Trade Descriptions Act 1968 makes it an offence to mis-describe your accommodation, facilities or approval. For instance, 'sea view' must be accurate as must 'all en suite bathrooms' and 'Tourist Board approved'.

THE BOURNE HOTEL

TARIFF — MARCH, APRIL, MAY & OCTOBER 2000

For *one* person	£25–£28	per night including VAT and full English breakfast.
	£37–£40	per night including VAT, full English breakfast and evening dinner.
For *two* persons	£34–£43	per night including VAT and full English breakfast.
	£54–£63	per night including VAT, full English breakfast and evening dinner.

Rooms with en suite bathroom and seaview — £4 extra per person per night.
No service charge made.
Mastercard and Visa credit cards accepted without surcharge.

Fig. 15. Tariff notice.

Should you offer food to non-residents either by way of bar snacks or restaurant meals, you need to display another notice that can be seen before those intending to eat reach the supply area. This is required under the **Price Marking (Food and Drink on Premises) Order 1979** with the object of allowing customers, while not under pressure, to see what the food and drink costs before they commit themselves.

Trading Standards Officers, who oversee these regulations, will provide you with literature setting out the information you need to include in notices.

DO YOU NEED STAFF?

Whereas in a manufacturing business it is wise to consider new staff in terms of increased production, in hotels extra staff will rarely increase turnover. You may be able to carry out a particular function better, or it may lessen someone else's workload, or it may free principals to do other things.

Assessment of needs

Since salaries and wages are frequently a hotelier's biggest outlay, you will be wise to consider in depth why you think you need an extra pair of hands and what the implications are:

- Do you require a special skill you feel you might not have the time or ability to carry out yourself?
- Do you have the time to train a new member of staff?
- Do you need someone extra all the time — or just at peak times?
- Can the employee carry out other duties when not engaged on the main task?
- Are you happy to let someone inexperienced loose on your guests?
- Can you really afford to take someone on?

Inevitably many employees do not work as hard nor as conscientiously as someone who derives direct profit from the business. It is sensible, therefore, to employ the absolute minimum you can. By studying the answers to the previous questions, you will be able to decide if you really need to take someone on. If the answer is 'Yes,' draw up a job description to show:

- the job title
- the purpose of the job
- the main tasks to be performed
- the duties
- any possible job development.

From the information you have listed, you will be able to decide whether you want full-time or part-time staff.

Although the procedure might seem a little cumbersome for taking someone on, for example, to wait on tables, it is a useful exercise each time you think of new staff.

When considering whether you need staff, bear in mind employment legislation is complicated, is becoming increasingly so, and is always liable to change. Hence the provision of Public Enquiry Points at most main offices of the Advisory, Conciliation and Arbitration Service (ACAS). Telephone numbers are in all local directories.

Taking on existing staff

Under the **Transfer of Undertakings (Protection of Employment) Regulations 1981**, as amended, you have no option but to take on existing staff under certain circumstances, since employees employed by the vendor automatically become employees of the new owner on the same terms and conditions. The situation, however, may not be straightforward. DTI booklet *Employment Rights on transfer of an undertaking* (PL699), obtainable from Jobcentres, may assist.

For clarification on specific sets of circumstances, you should speak to the appropriate regional office of ACAS, or consult your solicitor.

Recruiting new staff

Staff may be recruited through:

● the local Jobcentre
● local employment agencies
● local/national advertising
● word of mouth.

Trainees cost employers less than conventional members of staff but hoteliers are expected to have a commitment to training and, ideally, will themselves have a formal training qualification such as a **Craft Training Award**. Advice may be obtained from the Hospitality Training Foundation Helpline, 3rd floor, International House, High Street, Ealing, London W5 5DB, Tel: (09068) 443322, with offices throughout England, Wales and Scotland, and from some Universities and Colleges of Further Education.

Also the **Hotel & Catering Training Company,** (10th floor, 26–28 Hammersmith Grove, London W6 7HT, Tel: (020) 7735 9700. Fax: (020) 7735 9701. Web: www.hctc.co.uk) delivers youth and adult government-funded training programmes, *eg* Modern Apprenticeships, National Traineeships, and programmes supporting the New Deal. On-the-job skills are provided alongside formal training.

The local Careers Service or Jobcentre will assist if you wish to take on a young person.

You want to find the right person straight away, so think what you will expect from an employee, especially one who will come into direct contact with your guests. Remember that guests need to be impressed — you don't want a member of your staff to undo all the hard work you have put in to making their stay memorable.

To build up a picture of the sort of employees you want, consider:

● Their health — hotel work is arduous.
● Their appearance — do they look as *you* like a waiter, or whatever, to look?
● Their manner — guests need to be treated with respect.
● The way they talk. Guests must be able to understand what they say (but do not contravene the **Race Relations Act 1976**).
● Some experience may save you time training them.
● A good standard of education may help them to communicate more effectively.
● If over-qualified, they could easily get bored and might not stay.
● Is their personality suited to the job they will be doing?

In drafting an advertisement, which should be reasonably informal, state:

- the job title
- the wages offered
- your requirements — *eg* experience, educational and/or professional qualifications, any age restrictions and personal qualities.

The **British Hospitality Association** used to carry out a nationwide wages and salaries survey each year and may do so in the future. Very useful for finding out the going rate in a particular area.

Finally, make sure your advertisement does not contravene the law. You must not insist on any particular race or colour (**Race Relations Act 1976**) nor can you require only males or females or unmarried persons (**Sex Discrimination Act 1975**), or exclude women of child-bearing age.

Having drawn up a short list of maybe five or six candidates, assuming the response has been good, allocate as much time as you can for interviewing. You will not be able to assess candidates properly unless there is enough time to put them at their ease before the interview starts in earnest. Then give them sufficient time to answer questions and show you what they're made of.

Ask them, for instance, what do you find attractive about this position? What did you find unattractive about your last/present job? How do you see your future in catering? Your notebook and pen will be handy. All the time think of what *you* expect of a person in that position. Will the interviewee fit in with your other staff? Will your guests be impressed?

Since candidates often choose employers at interviews and you don't want to lose the best because you have failed to impress, make sure you are in a position to answer any questions you may be asked. Interviews should be two-way, not just a means of eliciting essential information from a cowed candidate. If you are to work together you will need a good rapport.

EMPLOYING STAFF

There are a number of points to bear in mind when you take on staff. But whatever your obligations in law, *you* are the one doing the employing, you are entitled to have the staff you want and you can get rid of staff who are unsatisfactory. You must, however, be fair.

Your commitment

The theme running like a thread through employment law today is fairness. Employees need to know what their contract of employment with you is, in other words what **terms** and **conditions** have been agreed between you. You are obliged to furnish an employee you keep for one month with a written statement within two months of starting work. It must include:

- The names of the employer and employee.
- The date when the employment began.
- If any previous employment counts as part of the period of continuous employment, the date it began.
- The rate of pay at a specific date.
- The intervals at which payment is made.
- Any terms and conditions relating to: hours of work; holiday pay (including entitlement on termination of employment); incapacity for work due to sickness/injury including payment; any pensions and pension schemes.
- Length of notice of termination to be given by each side.
- The job title or a job description.

Before attempting to write a statement, get DTI booklets PL700 and PL700A, obtainable from Jobcentres. They give full details, including a specimen statement.

Training
When you employ staff, you should look upon yourself as a continual trainer. Staff will take their lead from you and if you show the wrong attitude, so will they. If you find an employee doing something incorrectly, start by asking yourself the reason why. If staff are not told and/or shown the proper way to do a job, they will not know and you can't expect them to do things as you want them done.

Formal training for the sort of staff you might employ is provided by, among others, Colleges of Further Education. There have been schemes which allowed for training to be given free of charge and grants may be available. (Speak also to your local **Business Link**.) Training, formal or informal, is a prerequisite of efficiency.

Disciplinary procedures
Discipline is always a touchy subject. Recommended disciplinary practice and procedures are set out in the **ACAS Code of Practice** which is reproduced in DTI booklet *Individual Rights of Employees*. Through ACAS you can obtain a booklet *Discipline at Work*.

Employees' rights
These include time off to look for alternative work, the right to return to work after pregnancy, redundancy payments (if applicable), the right to complain of unfair dismissal and receiving written notice of the reasons for dismissal. Also covered are time off for dependents, time off for antenatal care, parental leave, maternity rights, and the right to be provided with a reasonable standard of health, safety and welfare. An employer's responsibilities in this respect also apply to your guests.

Health and safety
The Health and Safety at Work, *etc.* Act 1974 applies to the premises as well, *eg* the state of floor covering and electrical fittings, indeed anything which puts people at risk.

Some of the other provisions for you to think about are:

● If you employ anyone, you need to register with your Local Authority Environmental Health Department.

● Employees may not be required to work excessive hours or unsuitable shift patterns which may lead to ill health or accidents caused by fatigue. The **Working Time Regulations 1998** cover specifically working hours, rest breaks, weekly rest periods, shift patterns and annual leave entitlements. To avoid falling foul of this highly-complicated piece of legislation, you may alternatively, following set procedures, enter into a workforce agreement with your staff plus individual ones with those working more than 48 hours a week. Your Local Authority **Health & Safety Enforcement Officer** will tell you what the requirements are. A complete guide, produced by solicitors for employers, is available free to full members of the **British Hospitality Association**, also a booklet, *A Guide to Working Time Regulations*, may be obtained from the DTI, Tel: 0845 6000925.

● Employees should expect to be provided with proper protective clothing when handling harmful substances, *eg* some cleaning fluids. (These must be avoided if at all possible). Risks must be assessed and training given.

● Employees should avoid the need for hazardous manual handling (*eg* very heavy luggage) as far as reasonably practicable. Again, the risks must be assessed and training given.

● Employees may not be exposed to excessive noise. Yet again, the risks have to be assessed.

Although application of the Act is largely common sense, relevant booklets are available free from HSE Books (see below).

Under the **Health and Safety Information for Employees Regulations 1989**, either an up-to-date poster must be displayed or each employee must be handed a leaflet setting out basic information on health and safety. Posters and leaflets, both of which change from time to time, are obtainable from:

HSE Books
PO Box 1999
Sudbury
Suffolk CO10 6FS.
Tel: (01787) 881165.
Fax: (01787) 313995.
Web: www.open.gov.uk/hse/hsehome.htm

In addition, if five or more people are employed, a written **health and safety policy statement** must be produced. Though that may not apply to you, the **Workplace (Health, Safety and Welfare) Regulations 1992** do, and by the **Management of Health and Safety at Work Regulations 1999** you are obliged to assess all hazards and risks throughout your establishment. There is no obligation to record your findings if you have fewer than five employees, but it is strongly recommended that you do so.

Of particular interest are booklets *An Introduction to health and safety, Five steps to risk assessment, A guide to risk assessment requirements, Health and Safety in small firms*, and *Writing a safety policy statement*. These may be obtained from either HSE Books or from Environmental Health Officers, who will also give advice.

Accidents can and do occur in hotels, particularly in kitchens. As a hotelier, under the **Reporting of Injuries, Diseases and Dangerous Occurrences Regulations 1995**, you have certain duties:

- if anyone dies or is seriously injured in an accident in connection with your business, or
- if there is a dangerous occurrence, *eg* a cooker blowing up,

you must notify your local Environmental Health Department as soon as possible, usually by telephone.

Further:

- if anyone is off work for more than three days as the result of an accident at work, or

- if you have had to notify any death, serious injury or dangerous occurrence, or
- if a specified occupational disease (listed in a booklet *RIDDOR 95* obtainable from the EH Dept) is certified by a doctor,

you must send a report to the EH Dept within ten days. Reports must be on Form F2508 or, in the case of disease, on Form F2508A, obtainable from HSE Books (see page 107).

A record must be kept of all such occurrences.

For assistance, speak to an EHO or ring HSE's Infoline 0541 545500.

Payment

It is an offence to pay less than the statutory minimum wage (**National Minimum Wage Act 1998**) and, in most circumstances, to pay men and women different rates for the same job (**Equal Pay Act 1970**). Details of current rates and guidance with regard to the staff accommodation offset and the treatment of tips may be obtained from Jobcentres or by telephoning the National Minimum Wage Helpline on (0845) 6000678.

Each year in the Budget, a limit is set above which income tax and **National Insurance** contributions must be paid. If any of your employees earn more than these lower earnings limits, you are obliged by law to deduct tax and/or **National Insurance contributions** from their pay on behalf of the government under **Pay As You Earn** (PAYE).

For this reason you should notify the Inland Revenue as soon as you employ staff, even if their pay is below the limits. (This is in case they have other earnings you know nothing about.) You will be sent an **Employers' Starter Pack** which contains all the instructions, tables and forms you need to operate PAYE, to deduct NI contributions and to deal with sick and holiday pay. There is a national helpline for employers (0845 6070143) and another helpline (08457 143143) which assists with basic VAT registration enquiries.

Your obligations extend to collecting from employees a **Form P45** and to furnishing them with a payslip. In the absence of a **Form P45** you must send in a **Form P46**.

Your own record will be kept on **deductions working sheets** (Form P11), one for each employee. These must be retained for a minimum of three years and if you have only a few employees can serve as your only wages records.

The deductions are calculated from the tables you are sent and together with a payslip (obtainable in books from the Inland Revenue) you will send both tax and NI contributions to the Revenue by the 19th of the month following that in which the deductions are made.

At the end of each year, a **summary sheet** (Form P14) is made out in triplicate and the top two copies sent to the Revenue. The third copy is given to the employee as **Form P60**.

DISPOSING OF STAFF

Dismissal

There are five statutory grounds which would justify dismissal:

- conduct
- capability
- redundancy
- a statutory requirement
- some other substantial reason.

In all cases you must be seen to have acted fairly and, if you stick to the provisions of the ACAS Code of Practice, any subsequent tribunal hearing should find in your favour.

In certain circumstances when an employee resigns, you may still be deemed to have acted unfairly. This applies if you are considered to have forced the resignation by your conduct. It is termed 'constructive dismissal'.

Notice

Unless you sack someone on the spot for gross misconduct such as dishonesty, minimum periods of notice are laid down according to the length of time an employee has been with you:

- between one month and two years: one week
- two years: two weeks
- each extra year: one extra week to a maximum of 12.

Periods of notice may vary according to the contract between you. If you require an employee to give you more than one week's notice, get it included in the contract.

Redundancy

Employees may be dismissed on grounds of redundancy providing it is done fairly and without any other factors being taken into consideration.

The rules on redundancy and qualifying for payments are complicated and may be found in *Fair and Unfair Dismissal, Redundancy Consultation and Notification* and *Redundancy Payments* from the Employment Service, also *Redundancy Handling* from ACAS.

In brief, payments are made on the basis of complete years' service to persons qualifying. Limits are set annually.

OTHER EMPLOYMENT PROCEDURES

Over 30 booklets dealing with the various aspects of employment, in addition to those already mentioned, are available free of charge from Jobcentres and from ACAS.

A number of booklets including *Sex Discrimination Act and Advertising* and *Codes of Practice* are available from:

The Equal Opportunities Commission
Overseas House
Quay Street
Manchester M3 3HN.
Tel: (0161) 833 9244.
Fax: (0161) 835 1657
Email: info@eoc.org.uk

A Code of Practice is available from:
The Commission for Racial Equality
Elliot House
10-12 Allington Street
London SW1E 5EH
Tel: (020) 7828 7022.
Fax: (020) 7630 7605
Email:info@cre.gov.uk

Thinking of Taking Someone On? — *PAYE Tax and National Insurance Contributions for Employers* (CWL3), *Inspection and Examination of Business Accounts* (IR72), *Your Guide to Self Assessment* (SA/Book 8), and *Self Assessment* — *a general guide to keeping records* (SA/Book 4) are available from Inland Revenue offices.

CASE STUDY

Andrew and Christine Bright have taken on a staff of four. Pat and Jennie work as cleaner and waitress respectively, for 20 hours a week each. Both are entitled to receive a written contract of employment (which will include the period they worked for the vendor) and to receive the protection of the Employment Acts. Since there are fewer than 20 employees, an additional note is not required.

Maggie and Yvonne each work 12 hours a week as washers-up. On the purchase of a commercial dishwasher costing £2,400 inc VAT, they will be made redundant. The Bright's solicitor has advised that, since they have not worked a total of two continuous years, they are not entitled to redundancy payments. Their contracts of employment specified one week's notice.

The Brights have made an immediate purchase of a six-slice toaster, a hot water boiler and a fan-assisted refrigerator, costing a total of £1,010 including VAT.

CHECKLIST

- Do you know what regulations you need to comply with?
- Is your kitchen properly laid out and equipped?
- Are your public rooms comfortable and well furnished?
- Does your bar and equipment comply with the law?
- Do your bedrooms meet ETC standards?
- Have you considered upgrading them?
- Is your hotel generally well equipped?
- Have you considered leasing essential new equipment?
- Is the outside well lit and welcoming?
- Are your hotel sign and tariff clearly visible?
- Have you carefully assessed what staff you need?
- Do you know how to advertise for and recruit staff?
- Do you know how to administer and train staff?
- Do you know about PAYE and National Insurance?
- Do you know how to dispose of staff?
- Do you know your obligations in law?

7

Book-keeping and Accounts

VAT (VALUE ADDED TAX)

Since VAT is referred to throughout this chapter and elsewhere, it is worth dealing with at this stage so you can assess whether it does or should apply to you.

What is it?

It is a tax which is administered, some say with vigour, by HM Customs and Excise. It is levied on all 'taxable supplies' above a certain threshold.

Services for payment, which are what hoteliers provide, are classified as 'standard-rated taxable supplies'. The current standard rate is $17^1/_2$ per cent.

How does it work?

Every taxable person, viz an individual, partnership or company, who is or is required to be registered for VAT, must account for the tax when making a taxable supply. This tax is called **output tax**.

VAT charged to you on your business purchases is known as **input tax**.

At regular intervals, normally once a quarter, you will receive a VAT return (Form VAT 100) on which you will have to enter the output tax you have charged and the input tax you have been charged. If the output exceeds the input, you pay the difference. If the input exceeds the output, you claim the difference. Simple, isn't it? Don't you believe it!

A manual with supplements running to almost 200 pages and known as *The VAT Guide* answers all the 'but what ifs' and is obtainable free from your local VAT office.

You must of course maintain accurate records to enable you to complete the return. The form in which you keep them is not specified.

It is possible to alter the tax period normally adopted to fit in with your financial year. The system also allows you to take over the registration number of the outgoing hotelier. Although this has advantages, for example you may be able to opt for annual accounting straight away, it should be avoided since any liability found on that VAT number would become your responsibility.

Value Added Tax Return
For the period
to

31st March 1999

HM Customs
and Excise

For Official Use

Registration number | Period
121 2121 21 | 3 99

A A Bright

The Bourne Hotel
Surfbourne
SF91 5QT

You could be liable to a financial penalty
if your completed return and all the VAT
payable are not received by the due date.

Due date: 30th April 1999

For
official
use
D O R
only

SPECIMEN

Fold Here

Before you fill in this form please read the notes on the back and the VAT leaflet "Filling in your VAT return". Fill in all boxes clearly
in ink, and write 'none' where necessary. Don't put a dash or leave any box blank. If there are no pence write "00" in the pence column.
Do not enter more than one amount in any box.

For official use			£	p
	VAT due in the period on **sales** and other outputs	**1**	223	40
	VAT due in this period on **acquisitions** from other EC Member States	**2**	NONE	
	Total VAT due (the sum of boxes 1 and 2)	**3**	223	40
	VAT reclaimed in this period on **purchases** and other inputs (including acquisitions from the EC)	**4**	603	40
	Net VAT to be paid to Customs or reclaimed by you **(Difference between boxes 3 and 4)**	**5**	(380	00)
	Total value of **sales** and all other outputs excluding any VAT. **Include your box 8 figure**	**6**	1276	00
	Total value of **purchases** and all other inputs excluding any VAT. **Include your box 9 figure**	**7**	3448	00
	Total value of all **supplies** of goods and related services, excluding any VAT, to other **EC Member States**	**8**	NONE	00
	Total value of all **acquisitions** of goods and related services, excluding any VAT, from other **EC Member States**	**9**	NONE	00

Retail schemes. If you have used any of the schemes in the
period covered by this return, enter the relevant letter(s) in this box.

If you are enclosing
a payment please
tick this box.

DECLARATION: You, or someone on your behalf, must sign below.

I ANDREW ALAN BRIGHT declare that the
(Full name of signatory in BLOCK LETTERS)

information given above is true and complete.

Signature A A Bright Date 20/4 19 99

A false declaration can result in prosecution.

PCU Apr 1995

VAT 100 (Full)   12

Fig. 16. Typical VAT return

Liability to pay

If your business, or businesses, have a taxable turnover of more than the prevailing threshold for liability to pay VAT (in 2003/4 it was £56,000), you become a taxable person. (It is the person, known as a **registered person**, who is liable to pay VAT, not the business.)

If the business you are taking over has regularly turned over more than the threshold sum, registration to take effect on your takeover day is the obvious answer.

Otherwise, because from the date on which you are first required to be registered all taxable supplies you make are liable to VAT, you need to act promptly if it appears you may exceed the threshold. It is illegal to charge VAT before you have been allocated a number. Rules governing this situation are set out in the leaflet *Should I Be Registered for VAT?* obtainable from Customs and Excise. Severe penalties are applied if rules are broken.

Should I register voluntarily?

It will rarely be sensible to apply for registration if the law doesn't require you to. Very heavy starting-up costs would be needed to justify this course. Otherwise the tax erodes not only your competitiveness but also your profits and gives you a lot of paperwork to worry about.

An example

As is shown on the VAT return reproduced in Figure 16, because of the new equipment bought, Andrew Bright is due a refund of £380 in his first tax period. Providing his turnover is as forecast, he will be a net payer in succeeding periods. His business therefore derives no long-term benefit from being VAT-registered.

Special rules

Special rules peculiar to hotels apply if guests stay for a *continuous* period of more than four weeks. Without breaking this rule, long-term residents may take occasional weekends away or a holiday and students may go home for vacations if they return to the same accommodation the next term, or pay a retaining fee to reserve the accommodation.

In these circumstances, from the 29th day of the stay, VAT is not due on the accommodation charge. It must, however, be paid in full on meals, drinks and service, plus an extra amount, not less than 20 per cent of the remainder after meals, drinks and service have been deducted, for facilities. An example of how this works is shown in Figure 17.

The reduced value rules do *not* apply to block bookings by tour operators, airlines, companies and other organisations where accommodation is used by a succession of short-stay residents.

VAT Calculations

A   Total tax-inclusive charge for first four weeks   £141.00

B   Tax-inclusive charge for meals (£50 plus VAT
    at $17^1/_2\%$)   £58.75
C   Tax-exclusive charge for meals   £50.00

D   Tax-inclusive charge for accommodation &
    facilities (A-B)   £82.25
E   Tax included in D   £12.25
                                                         _____

F   Balance, exclusive of tax   £70.00
G   Tax-exclusive value of facilities (not less than
    20% of the balance)   £14.00

H   Total tax VAT due on £14.00   £2.45
                                                         _____

                                                          £11.20

The weekly terms are therefore £120.00 (C+F)
plus £11.20 VAT   =   £131.20

Fig. 17. How to work out the reduced tax value for accommodation exceeding
four weeks, when your charges are expressed in tax-inclusive terms.

The rules governing VAT are always liable to change. The up-to-date
situation can be ascertained by getting the booklets applicable to your
situation from the local VAT office. In addition to those already mentioned, you may find *Hotels and holiday accommodation, Records and
accounts* and *Transfer of a going concern* of interest.

KEEPING THE BOOKS

Accountants
Although you can prepare accounts yourself, and after reading this chapter you will at least be able to understand how it is done, the process is
very time-consuming and requires a lot of expertise to get it right. Tax
rules change with amazing rapidity and an accountant well versed in
hotel businesses will save you much time and worry.

By claiming everything it is possible to set against tax, an accountant's fees can easily be less than the tax you have legally avoided paying.

If you should come up against an over-zealous tax inspector it is a comfort to know you have someone on your side acting as a buffer. If you are doing your own accounts, unless properly qualified, you can be caused a lot of worry. You need to be able to concentrate all your efforts on making profits.

Just a word of warning. If, after initially assuring you that your accounts would be dealt with personally, you find your accountant is not au fait with your affairs through delegating to unqualified juniors, do not hesitate in issuing the order of the boot. The charges are far too high for you to put up with a second-rate service. You must have an accountant you can trust completely and talk to easily when you need advice.

Data to be recorded

The minimum data you are required by law to keep is enough to enable you to complete your VAT return, if registered, and wages information on Forms P11 if you have employees. It has been known for those in business to throw all copies of invoices and receipts in the direction of their accountant with the comment, 'It's what we pay him for!'

And pay you will if that's the system you adopt! Not only in cash terms but because you will never be in a position to complete the 'actual' columns of your cashflow and budget forecasts. This is the information you need if you are going to keep control over your finances to make sure everything is going according to plan. Financial control is all-important.

Where should it be recorded?

The simplest way of recording data is in one of the many printed books sold for the purpose. Some are better than others but, because every business is different, there are always columns you don't need and some you want which aren't there.

Bearing in mind the guidance your accountant also gives you, have a look at a simple method which will suit most hoteliers.

A couple of general rules regarding VAT:

- If you are VAT-registered, divorce VAT from all relevant amounts except when recording cashflow.
- If not registered, record all expenditure as the amount you are charged, whether or not there is a VAT element.

Purchase an A4-size book with lines and rule up pages opposite each other, the left-hand one headed '**Income**', the one on the right '**Expenditure**'.

On the left under Income, the columns should be headed:

- Date
- Invoice number
- Name/source
- Gross amount received
- Basic amount (only if VAT-registered)
- VAT element (only if VAT-registered)
- How paid (*eg* cheque/cash)
- Date paid to bank
- Date to cash.

Under Expenditure on the right-hand page rule up the following columns:

- Receipt no. (all invoices/receipts to be given a consecutive number each financial period)
- Payee
- Cheque/cash (if cheque, record the number)
- Total amount
- Basic amount (if VAT-registered)
- VAT element (if VAT-registered)
- Purpose, *eg* motor – petrol
- Bank balance
- Cash balance.

Examples of this type of record, showing the date of transaction in the extreme left-hand column, are shown in Figures 18 and 19. By entering all outgoings from the bank, *eg* direct debits on the due dates, you can always tell what your balance is.

Divide your records into weeks, if you want that sort of tight control, but definitely keep the months separate. This will enable you to end up with monthly totals for your cashflow and profit forecast forms. Leave space at the end of each month for summaries:

- Gross income
- Basic income (if VAT-registered)
- VAT element (if VAT-registered)
- Amount paid into bank
- Cash retained (for business purposes).

INCOME RECORD

Date	Invoice No.	Name/Source	Gross Amount	Basic Amount	VAT	How Paid	Date to Bank	Date to Cash
6/3	101	Parkinson	59.60	50.72	8.88	Cheque	9/3	
6/3	102	Newman	30.00	25.53	4.47	Cheque	9/3	
6/3	–	Bar	12.50	10.64	1.86	Cash	–	6/3
7/3	103	Smith	127.90	108.85	19.05	Visa	9/3	
9/3	–	Phone box	18.20	15.49	2.71	Cash		9/3
Total for March			6000.00	5106.38	893.62			

Fig. 18. Example of income record.

Within the Income and Expenditure sections you have sufficient information if you need to compile a VAT return:

- VAT payable (output tax) on taxable supplies, less any understatement in earlier returns (£1,000 limit without reference to the VAT office).
- VAT claimed (input tax) on business purchases, less any understatement as above.
- Net amount payable or reclaimed.
- Value of outputs (income) excluding VAT.
- Value of inputs (expenditure) excluding VAT.

Remember to make adjustments for any credits you might make or receive.

Although you can duplicate wages information, it really is not necessary with a small number of employees as the **deductions working sheets** kept in a suitable binder are the only record you need keep.

Preferably every week, transfer the information in your Expenditure section on to analysis sheets (found in large stationers). These are already ruled into columns for you to insert the headings.

EXPENDITURE RECORD								
Receipt No.	Payee	Cheq/ Cash	Total Amount	Basic Amount	VAT	Purpose	Bank Balance	Cash Balance
							49.80	23.50
12	RJ Smith	Cash	19.60			Provs. Grn Groc		3.90
13	I Lowes	626	36.20	30.81	5.39	Repairs Elec	13.60	16.40
							231.10	34.60
			5475.01	410.11	71.77		525.60	50.21

Fig. 19. Example of expenditure record.

Suggested headings are:

- Date
- The first four (or six if VAT-registered) columns under Expenditure above, followed by:
- Provisions
- Rates (plus any rent)
- Heat and light
- Insurance
- Motor and travel
- Telephone
- Cleaning and household
- Printing, postage, stationery, advertising
- Repairs and renewals
- Bank charges
- Professional fees/licences
- Cash drawings (amounts taken out of the business)
- Capital items (*eg* new equipment)
- Miscellaneous.

Invoices
For ease of control, make out an invoice in duplicate each time you

receive other than small amounts of cash, *eg* for bar snacks, drinks and so on. All invoices should be consecutively numbered for identification purposes and the number entered on the back of cheques received, also on credit card vouchers for easy identification.

If you are VAT-registered, the numbering is mandatory, the invoice is termed a '**tax invoice**' and must contain the following information:

- your VAT registration number
- your name and address
- the date of supply
- your customer's name and address
- the type of supply and description of the services, *eg* 'deposit on hotel booking 3rd to 17th August 200X'
- the charge made for each description, excluding VAT
- the total charge made, excluding VAT
- the rate of VAT
- the rate of any cash discount offered, *eg* '5 per cent discount for full settlement one month before booking taken up'
- the total VAT payable.

A specimen tax invoice is shown in Figure 20.

It is a good idea for tight control to endorse every invoice, including the copy, with the payment details, *eg* 'paid by Visa 17/8/XX' and sign it.

The importance of keeping meticulous records

Apart from maintaining financial control and supplying accurate information to your accountant, it's important to keep meticulous records because you could be subject to:

- a visit by a VAT officer
- an investigation by the Inland Revenue.

VAT officers visit places of business where the tax is in issue as a matter of course, to ensure you understand VAT and are applying the rules properly. The officer will examine your business records, methods and premises to check that your returns are accurate. Transgressions may be punished with penalties.

For various reasons, your business could be subjected to an 'in-depth' investigation by a tax inspector. The less complete your records, the more difficult it will be to convince the inspector you are paying the right amount of tax.

Both VAT officers and tax inspectors have extensive powers in requiring additional information and documentation. Dishonesty is

Invoice No. 999   22nd March 200X

THE BOURNE HOTEL

The Esplanade
Surfbourne SF91 5QT
Tel: (01999) 121212

Mr. A. Discerning
3 London Road
London W6   Tax point 22/3/0X

To:
Dinner, bed and breakfast
15th to 22nd March 200X
2 persons @ £160.86   321.72
Bar purchases   63.25
Laundry   12.50
                                                  _____
                                                  397.47
                   VAT @ 17^1/2%   69.56

                   TOTAL   **467.03**

Received cheque No. 555666
with thanks.

_____

Resident Proprietors Mr. & Mrs. A. Bright
VAT Reg'd No. 121 2121 21

Fig. 20. How to make out an invoice.

punished ruthlessly.

ACCOUNTS

Unless you run a limited company, in which case your books have to be audited, your accountant can only produce a set of accounts from the information you provide. If your account book, analysis sheets and wages records are kept meticulously, everything should be straightforward.

Trading and profit and loss account.

From the information you provide, a trading and profit and loss account will be prepared. In normal circumstances, for comparison purposes, the figures will be shown alongside those for the previous year.

An example

The Trading and Profit and Loss Account for the Bourne Hotel after one year's trading and using figures similar to those in the cashflow and budget projections will look like the one in Figure 21. VAT is not in issue but would be included were the Brights not registered. Their accountant has advised they include Cleaning and Household Sundries and Miscellaneous as separate columns. This is reflected in the accounts and in the headings shown under Expenditure on page 119.

Balance sheet

Your accountant will also draw up a balance sheet together with a schedule which will detail your fixed assets.

Each year, the **depreciation** on your assets that wear out is assessed. Typically, this is the value of the item when new or introduced into the business divided by the number of years you expect it to last.

Cars are usually written off at 20 per cent per annum on a reducing balance basis, so that there is always some value left in it. A car worth £6,000, for example, will have £1,200 written off its value after a year. The next year, its revised value of £4,800 will have 20 per cent, that is £960 written off to leave a value of £3,840, and so on.

The residue of your assets after an allowance for depreciation on machinery, equipment and motor vehicles used in the business will appear on the balance sheet as Fixed Assets as per Schedule.

The other headings used in balance sheets are shown in Figure 22.

In addition to these accounts, a pool or pools will be formed which include **capital allowances**, not to be confused with depreciation. Current rules, which are liable to change, allow for 25 per cent of capital

MR & MRS A BRIGHT — TRADING AS 'THE BOURNE HOTEL'

TRADING AND PROFIT AND LOSS ACCOUNT
YEAR ENDING 31ST DECEMBER 200X

	£	£
Takings		89470
Own consumption and accommodation		3600
		93070
Cost of takings		
Opening stock	520	
Provisions	22210	
	22730	
Less: Closing stock	580	
		22150
Gross Profit		70920
Expenses		
Wages	7900	
Rates	2715	
Heat and Light	2830	
Insurance	600	
Motor and Travel	990	
Telephone	1050	
Cleaning and Household	780	
Printing/postage/stationery/ads	4250	
Repairs and Renewals	790	
Banking and Finance charges	8050	
Professional fees/licences	1950	
Cash drawings	14000	
Miscellaneous	170	
Depreciation	4140	50215
Net profit		20705

Fig. 21. Example of a Trading and Profit and Loss Account.

expenditure on 'plant and machinery', which includes equipment used exclusively for your business to be used in each year as tax relief. (The current ceiling on cars is £12,000, viz £3,000 pa.)

Your accountant will use these **capital**, or **writing-down allowances**, only if you are liable to pay tax in the current year, in other words, if you are making a profit. They will otherwise be carried forward, either wholly or in part, until you have income to set them against.

This is the way in which you get tax relief on capital items you buy for the business. Those items leased to you are a business expense and do not attract capital allowances (except for the owner). Ask your accountant to keep you fully appraised of what is in the pool/s.

A special capital allowance of 4 per cent pa applies to the construction, extension or improvement of hotels with ten or more letting bedrooms. To qualify, the guests must change, there must be a bedmaking and cleaning service, and breakfast and evening meals must be provided. Other rules, which your accountant can advise you about, also apply. There may also be a VAT advantage. VAT leaflet 708/2 *Construction Industry* will tell you more.

INCOME TAX

What's your obligation?

As a self-employed person, you are liable to pay tax under **Schedule D**. This means you pay on what is known as a 'preceding year basis'.

How can an accountant help?

This is where a good accountant really comes into his own. Such an accountant will:

- Tell you the items you can legally set against tax. Claiming for ridiculous things like holidays on the basis you are drumming up business does nothing to enhance the relationship between you and the tax man.
- Complete your tax returns.
- Answer any queries raised by the Revenue and negotiate on your behalf (referring to you only if necessary).
- Lodge an appeal if an assessment appears too high.
- Ensure you pay not a penny more tax than you need to.

But you must do your bit by:

BALANCE SHEET

Fixed Assets as per schedule   £

Current assets
  Stock   £
  Debtors and prepayments   £
  Bank balance   £
  Cash in hand   £_____
                          £_____

Current liabilities
  Creditors   £
  Bank overdraft   £_____
                           £_____

Net Current Assets   £_____
                                          £_____

Long term liabilities
  Bank loan   £_____
Total Assets   £_____

Represented by:
  Capital introduced   £
  Add profit for year   £_____
                           £_____
Less drawings   £_____

                                          £_____
                                          _____

Fig. 22. The Headings on a Balance Sheet.

- Keeping records meticulously.
- Supplying them to your accountant promptly.
- Being completely honest.

You will find a tax bill comes in pretty promptly after your first year's trading, as an estimate if completed accounts have not been submitted. It is normally payable in two chunks, on 31 January and 31 July each year.

Once you have notified the Revenue you have started in business (see page 85) and the address of your accountant, copies of assessments will be sent there as well.

Some of you, particularly in smaller concerns, will make a loss in your first and maybe your second year. Losses can be set against any other income or carried forward to be set against future profits. Seek your accountant's advice.

In a partnership, tax is worked out much as for a sole trader but with responsibility divided according to the agreement entered into. The snag is that, should one partner default, the other/s are liable for the defaulter's share.

Where one or more partners have other income, each may be taxed at different rates, leading to complications if one defaults. If other income is received, seek advice.

Under present rules, if your gross business takings are less than £15,000 pa, instead of sending in detailed accounts you need only tell your tax inspector:

- your gross business takings or earnings, including any commission or tips
- your total business purchases and expenses
- your profits (or losses).

NATIONAL INSURANCE

Your obligation to pay

As a self-employed person, you are liable to pay Class 2 and 4 NI contributions.

- **Class 1 contributions** are paid by employed persons, as explained on page 108. If you are employed, *eg* a director of a company, as well as being self-employed, you must pay them in addition to your other obligations up to a set limit.

- **Class 2 contributions** are paid by people of less than retirement age. Payments may be made by monthly direct debit or quarterly billing. Contributors are entitled to certain benefits, *eg* sickness. Should you estimate your profits to be less than a ceiling set each year, (£4,095 in 2003/4) you may apply for a certificate of exception. Refunds of contributions are now possible but with set time limits. All is explained in DSS leaflet CA02, *National Insurance Contributions for Self-Employed people with small earnings*, and there is a helpline on 0645 154655.

- **Class 3 contributions** are voluntary and are designed to help individuals to qualify for retirement pension or widows' benefits. A booklet, *National Insurance Voluntary Contributions*, explains.

- **Class 4 contributions**, only for the self-employed, are profit-related and are generally assessed and collected by the Inland Revenue along with income tax. The booklet *National Insurance Contributions for Self-Employed Persons* explains Class 2 and 4 fully. Currently, half of Class 4 contributions qualify for tax relief.

There are circumstances in which it may be beneficial to apply for deferment of contributions, another area where a competent accountant's advice should be sought.

PENSIONS

It is never too early to plan for the future. State retirement pensions are traditionally miserly and you may have become accustomed to a standard of living unattainable on such a low income.

It is not sensible to rely on the sale of your assets to provide you with a comfortable living for the rest of your life. Circumstances change and disasters occur. A recession may mean you cannot sell your business when you planned to. If your health has let you down and you cannot sell, you may have to pay someone to run the hotel for you. In extreme cases, you may have to close down and become unable to service your borrowings. You could then go bankrupt.

Unless you are aged 50 or over, or retire on health grounds, Capital Gains Tax may erode the value of your hotel more than you had expected (see Inland Revenue booklet *Capital Gains Tax — an Introduction*). So unless you have an adequate index-linked pension from a previous employer, you should take out a pension plan to secure your future. No one can take a personal pension away from you and the chances of a major pension provider going to the wall are remote.

To encourage you to plan for your future, the government allows tax relief on what you pay into a pension plan (with certain limits) at your highest rate of tax. The percentage of your net earnings allowable for relief changes according to your age.

Types of pension plan are continually changing and it is impossible for *anyone* to recommend a particular type without knowing the exact circumstances. The expertise of financial intermediaries varies widely; some are excellent and, most importantly, honest. Others think only of the considerable commission to be earned on selling a pension plan.

Financial advisors fall into two categories:

1. Representatives of companies which may be:
    a. appointed representatives, or
    b. tied agents.
    This category, which your bank manager or insurance broker may fall into, may deal with only one company's products.

2. Independent.
    This category can, in theory, recommend any company product. In practice, this is not so since some companies, including household names, operate only with a direct sales force and have no facility for providing intermediaries with full details of their products.

When you are taking such a major step, you are entitled to know *precisely* who you are dealing with. Although by law you should be informed at the outset, this does not always happen.

Questions to ask:

*   What category of financial advisor are you?
*   If appointed representative or tied agent: Which company do you represent?
*   If independent: How many company products can you provide full information on?

Before embarking on a scheme:

*   Do not rush into anything. In particular, do not consider a pension until you know your business is going to be profitable. (Otherwise how can you pay the premiums?)
*   Once sure you will make a profit, do not delay.

- Speak to your accountant — ask if an 'executive' pension might be suitable for you.
- See your trusted financial advisor. This may be your insurance broker, bank manager or someone recommended to you by your accountant.
- Obtain details of the various schemes offered.
- Carefully assess the information and the implications.
- Do not consider a plan without waiver of premium cover. (This takes care of premiums if you are incapacitated.)
- Don't sign anything unless you are 100 per cent sure it's what suits your situation *precisely* and you have *absolute* confidence in the intermediary.
- Finally give your accountant full details of what you have been offered and get full approval of your choice.

CHECKLIST

Do you know:

- A good accountant?
- How VAT works?
- How to complete a VAT return?
- Why you have to keep records?
- What records you must keep?
- How you are going to keep records?
- How to keep control of your finances?
- How to complete analysis sheets?
- How to understand your accounts?
- Your obligations re income tax and National Insurance?
- How to go about getting a pension plan?

If you have five or more employees, you must, by law, provide them with access to a pension scheme.

8

Tariffs, Costs and Advertising

WHAT SHOULD WE CHARGE?

The simple answer is as much as the customer is willing to pay. This, however, is governed by three main factors:

- the existing tariff (if taking on a going concern)
- what your competitors are charging
- what you need to make a profit.

When you take on a hotel already trading, you will have an opinion as to the level of prices charged. Even if you think they're too low, you will still encounter some would-be guests who will express amazement at how high they are!

Unless the tariff is ridiculously low, it would be unwise (and maybe unlawful if you had already quoted prices) to immediately raise the rates. You would lose any chance of securing some of your predecessor's trade.

Even if you *know* your prices are too low, if you exceed the going rate charged by the hotels around it will reduce your business, perhaps crucially, no matter how good or up-market your facilities.

Hence the importance of choosing your location carefully in the first instance, especially if you want to offer superior facilities. It is always better to have an inferior property in an up-market location than a superior one in a less desirable area. Remember what estate agents say about the importance of location? They can't all be wrong!

If you are on your own, or at least have no close neighbours as competitors, you have more latitude. You will still need to find out what hotels similar to your own are charging, since would-be guests hunt through guides and other advertisements to make comparisons.

How do you calculate a tariff?

In a service industry it is more difficult to work out what you need to make a profit than if you are manufacturing something. Obviously the amount of provisions used will vary according to the number of guests, but most other overheads vary to a lesser extent. When you are open for business you can suddenly fill up — or remain empty.

You will already have prepared a forecast of earnings for the cashflow and profit projections. By:

- calculating a level of trade as on page 70
- looking at your break-even figure as on page 75
- reducing your 'drawings' figure to a minimum,

you can work out a percentage reduction on the tariff levels you originally worked to.

CASE STUDY

Andrew and Christine Bright's break-even figure is £62,643. If they reduced their own drawings by half, their overheads would be £41,235. Multiplying this amount by 100 and dividing by their gross profit margin (77 per cent) produces a revised break-even figure of £53,552, a percentage reduction of 14.5 per cent. As a rough guide, the tariff shown on page 101 could then be reduced by over 40 per cent. In those circumstances, no profit would be made and no money could be reinvested or put by for emergencies.

Providing you know the *minimum* you need to charge, taking into account all other considerations, calculate your tariff above that figure.

Some of the other considerations

Since advertising space in guides has to be bought months in advance, you will always need to fix the following year's tariff well in advance. As a rule of thumb, increase your prices each year in line with estimated inflation, allowing a couple of per cent leeway. Bearing in mind the facilities you offer, if you think your prices are still lower than the market can stand, add a few per cent until you feel you've got it right.

You will soon know how accurate your calculations are by the level of take-up from passing trade and advertisements, and comments made by your guests. Whatever the standard of your accommodation, it is important to give value for money.

Never advertise different tariffs in the same year's guides, nor charge more than you quoted (except for VAT increases). Some hoteliers put a warning on their tariffs that prices may be increased. Would *you* take that sort of chance as a guest? Nor will *your* guests. Fix your tariff, then stick to it. This also applies when someone calls and tries to get you to reduce your prices for them. To accede wouldn't be fair to those already in residence. If all hoteliers gave such people short shrift, they wouldn't try it. It is an increasing trend, particularly when the economy is not buoyant.

VAT

The subject has been discussed fully in Chapter 7, except for actually working it out.

Various examples are given in the VAT guide. The following are using the current rate of 17 $1/2$ per cent.

- To calculate standard rate VAT on a VAT-exclusive price, multiply by 17 $1/2$ per cent, *eg* £150 x 17 $1/2$ per cent = £26.25.

- To calculate the basic amount in a VAT-inclusive price, divide the total by 1 as a whole number plus the rate of VAT as a percentage, *eg* £300/1.175 = £255.32.

- To calculate the VAT element in a VAT-inclusive price, multiply the total by the rate of tax and divide by 100 plus the rate of tax, *ie* 17.5/117.5, which equates with 7/47. For example, £300 x 7/47 = £44.68.

When faced with fractions of pence, it is simplest (and permissible) to round to the nearest whole penny, *eg* 6.6p may be shown as 7p and 6.4p as 6p.

Variations in tariff

In considering variations, you will need to assess the type of guests you can expect. If wholly or mainly business, no variations would be either appropriate or necessary, except perhaps for attracting others at weekends when business people have gone home.

If wholly or mainly holiday trade, many people look for low-season reductions. By attracting this sort of trade, you will be extending your trading period. Christmas, New Year and to an extent Easter attract a premium since you will need to pay staff top rates.

Overnight stays are less profitable than longer ones since they involve a complete change of bed linen and thorough cleaning of wardrobes, drawers and so on. If your normal trade involves mainly overnight stays, the tariff should be geared to account for the extra expense. If not, you may consider a surcharge is justified. Your tariff could show either 'a reduction for two nights or more', or '£1.50 inc. VAT per person surcharge for single night stays'. The former is better since guests think they are getting a discount.

Discounts

Should you offer discounts as an incentive in abnormally quiet periods? 'Free accommodation for children' or 'three nights for the price of two' smack of panic measures if they are not your normal policy. Be careful not to give that impression (even if it is the case!), although you may need to respond to snap offers made by neighbours. Remember that in any type of price war, once you get below the tariff it is viable for you to charge, you may as well shut up shop and save yourself the effort.

In any circumstances, it is important (except as shown below) not to have some guests paying different rates to others. If those paying full rate find out, unpleasantness can result. At the least, they will not return.

Loyalty discounts are a different matter. All hotel businesses benefit enormously from repeat bookings. Why not reward those who contribute substantially to your well-being by giving them a discount? From calculations you have already made you will know what margin you have to play with.

What would be your reaction if you were offered a five per cent discount on future bookings once you had stayed three, five or seven nights? If everything else was right, it might tip the balance in favour of returning as opposed to going somewhere else. Guests thrive on knowing they are being treated as someone special, and such a gesture will help you build up a nucleus of regular guests — and save you a lot of money on formal advertising. It can therefore be self-financing.

Devise your own scheme for regulars. Maybe they could build up 'credits' until they have stayed a total of seven or even 14 nights to qualify for a discount. A couple bringing new guests might get an extra couple of per cent. Don't make things too complicated, but a carefully thought out scheme for guests to become members of the 'club' will easily justify the extra record-keeping, and quickly get you a list of regulars who will spread the word to friends and relatives. Each Christmas, send 'club' members a card together with the following year's brochure and tariff and a brief friendly message. Then watch how quickly your new family grows. Many will become real friends, not just guests.

Discount for children

You will have to think about discounts for youngsters. Everyone else does it, so if you take families you will have to follow suit. Maybe no accommodation charge would be made for under-2s. Other children sharing their parents' room could perhaps qualify for 40 per cent.

Any discount for those aged 12 and over would be purely a gesture, not a reflection of the lower costs incurred. Not only do such youngsters often eat more than their parents, they are far more finicky and could well cost you *more*. Be guided by your own situation, the practices of competitors around you and the experience of your new friends in the Hotels Association.

Bar prices

Hotel bar prices generally tend to be unnecessarily high. Profit margins are excellent, particularly for the small hotelier who, without brewery ties, can buy wines and spirits at lowest prices. Take, for example a standard 70cl bottle of whisky. Using a standard 25ml optic (more about this in Chapter 9), the bottle contains 28 measures. Multiply by what your local charges for a measure of whisky and you will be able to calculate the gross profit.

Although selling beer is not so lucrative, there is still sufficient margin, even taking into account wastage through spillage, pipe cleaning and so on to make a handsome profit.

Why, then, drive your guests away by hitting up your prices? If guests think you are charging way over the top, they will drink elsewhere.

Bearing in mind the margins, a scientific approach is not required. Go to a couple of locals, make a note of their prices (from the list that by law has to displayed) and fix your own just below, the same or fractionally above, depending on your clientele.

Making ten pence a measure less than your competitors could make the difference between an empty bar and a full one.

Beware of **happy hours**. Be prepared for guests who walk in late and argue your watch is fast, and others who appear for the cheap drinks and not at any other time.

By all means have special offers, particularly if you need to move a line that is fast approaching its sell-by date. Or you may have bought in a few cases of wine that were on special offer to you. But think carefully about 'happy hours'. They may work for you — they may not.

Holiday insurance

People taking a package holiday abroad have to be insured. Yet for many in the UK, insurance is far from their minds.

When someone makes a booking with you, it is a contract in law. If it is not honoured, even for the best of reasons, and there is no insurance in force, unless you are prepared to enforce the liability in the courts you could lose out. Remember it is your livelihood, and much as you may feel sorry for a family whose car crashes on their way to you for a fortnight's holiday, putting them in hospital, your bills might not get paid if you can't re-let the accommodation.

A number of insurance companies offer cost-effective cover for the major risks, such as death, illness, injury, redundancy and jury service. Wider cover, *eg* for luggage and personal effects, may be an optional extra.

Since cancellations are bound to occur, if you wish to avoid unpleasantness it is up to you to educate your guests as to their liabilities and, one way or another, do your best to see they are insured. In the first instance speak to your insurance broker and see what is on offer. A scheme is available for members of the **British Hospitality Association**, and your local Association may have negotiated competitive rates with a broker or an insurance company.

You have four options as far as holiday cancellation insurance is concerned:

- Ignore it, keep your fingers crossed and hope not too many guests cancel their bookings.
- Point out guests' obligations in law and leave any action up to them.
- Provide guests with a proposal form and a recommendation to take out cover.
- Be more direct, ask for their cooperation and build the cost into your tariff.

Putting a carefully worded statement on your booking confirmation forms or on a slip that you can stick to the bottom of your confirmation letter works well. See page 151 for an example that may work for you.

Remember, the contract also binds you to fulfill your obligation to provide accommodation.

Deposits

If there is time for a deposit to reach you before guests are due to arrive, ask for one. Make it sufficient for them to miss it if they should cancel. Ten per cent with a minimum of £20 per guest is reasonable. Not only does it show commitment on the part of the guest but it helps you with cash flow. Deposits that help you buy in provisions or stop you going into overdraft are beneficial. How to deal with and acknowledge deposits is dealt with in Chapter 9.

Settlement of accounts

No matter how much you might like being a hotelier, this is what you're in business for. Your object must be to get the money in as early as possible and with as much security as you can arrange. A cheque of the rubber variety (and there are plenty about) handed over on the last day of a fortnight's stay is of no use to you at all, particularly if the booking was casual. So what can you do to improve the situation?

Some guests don't like paying money up front. Yet it is reasonable to expect them to give you the opportunity to clear their cheques before they leave. A request to this effect on the booking confirmation (see Chapter 9) would be sensible.

A cheque guarantee card helps only if it covers the whole bill. If not, and the bank gets to know it, a number of cheques each not exceeding the card limit and made out in respect of one transaction may not be honoured if there are insufficient funds in the account.

A pre-authorisation facility has been introduced by **Certegy Limited**, a multi-national company. One free telephone call, made when a guest registers, indicates payment is desired by cheque and deposits a signed cheque with you, will, in most cases, guarantee the cheque will be honoured. The service can also be used by arrangement for business cheques.

Through **Cheque-In**, a charge of between one and two per cent of each cheque value is made for the service, plus a monthly subscription of £15 (£10 in the first year for members of the **British Hospitality Association**). All charges are plus VAT. Details are available by telephoning free 0800 626979.

Credit cards
Taking credit cards is another safe way of getting paid. *Providing you stick rigidly to the rules*, the service, which costs between one and four per cent depending on turnover, guarantees you will get your money even if the card has been stolen. (The **British Hospitality Association** negotiates advantageous credit card rates for its members.)

By the **Credit Cards (Price Discrimination) Order 1990**, merchants (those under contract to the credit card companies) are now at liberty to make a surcharge for payments made by credit card (or an adjustment for payments by cash). Any price differential has to be notified to the customer in accordance with the **Price Indications (Method of Payment) Regulations 1991**, by a notice at the public entrance and at points where payment is made.

COSTS AND OVERHEADS

Many of your costs and overheads have been mentioned in Chapter 7 but more detail on some may be helpful.

Banking
Running a business bank account is not cheap. Bank managers used to have wide discretion, but it is now common for them to be instructed to recover the total cost of running accounts from the customer.

The best you can hope for is to find a bank that goes easier than the others on small business users and will entice you into opening an account by offering free banking for maybe the first year. Get a complete list of charges from a number of banks and compare terms. Your choice is obviously limited if you have been loaned money by a particular bank.

Managers will offer most business users an overdraft facility to cater for sudden surges in expenditure and emergencies. Never exceed your limit or lapse into unauthorised overdraft; the charges are steep and it destroys the manager's confidence in the way in which you run your business.

Hotel Association membership

Many local associations are affiliated to the **British Hospitality Association** or to the **National Council of Hotel Associations**. They exist to provide support for members and to promote higher standards of accommodation. They are non-profit-making and keep fees to a minimum.

For a modest subscription you can have an accumulated wealth of knowledge at the end of a telephone. Some arrange discounts with local suppliers and may organise social events at quiet times of the year. Apart from assistance when you're looking for a hotel in a particular area, membership is well worth considering once you become a hotelier.

Professional fees

These are a way of life for almost all businesses. As long as you're not on the telephone every five minutes, which would bump the charges up, let the trained professional take the strain while you concentrate on making profits. All such fees are claimable against tax, as are the membership fees of trade associations.

The larger trade associations offer a range of professional services for their members and represent the views of the industry in Parliament and with various bodies which come into contact with hotels. Trade magazines and newsletters keep their readers up to date with new developments and changes in legislation.

Staff

The mechanics of employing staff is dealt with in Chapter 6. Two further points to think about:

- If you are employing staff on a regular, long-term basis, consider formal training for them. It ensures professionalism and gives them pride in their work. Part-time courses are run by Colleges of Further

Education. Their Hotel and Catering Departments usually have a restaurant which is open on a limited basis to the public. Go and investigate. See what they can do for your staff — and maybe for you!

● If yours is a very small establishment but you need some help, maybe someone living nearby would be prepared to do laundry, ironing, cutlery cleaning and so on at home. Worth investigating to reduce your burden and keep down costs.

Rates

Water and sewage services are charged the same as for domestic properties, *ie* based on rateable value, although change is planned. It is policy that all commercial properties should be metered. When that is a requirement of the water company, the company may bear the cost. It varies from area to area.

Business rates, applicable to all hotels, *etc* which take more than six paying guests, or where the business is assessed as not being subsidiary to the domestic situation, are fixed on a national basis. The rate is assessed on how much the property could have been rented for on 1 April 1993 and is reassessed every five years thereafter. Such valuations are carried out by a Valuation Officer of the Inland Revenue.

● The amount payable is calculated by multiplying the rateable value by the national uniform rate (for 2003/4, 44.4p in the £). Typically, a small hotel with a rateable value of £4,000 will currently be charged £1,776.

Additionally, the owners are liable to pay **Council Tax**, fixed locally according to specific bands, on the part of the premises they occupy exclusively for their own use and where business rates are not levied.

A range of leaflets explaining the Business Rate is available free from:

Department of the Environment
DETR Free Literature
PO Box 236
Wetherby LS23 7NB
Tel: (0870) 122 6236
Fax: (0870) 122 6237

Miscellaneous

The various costs of licences, *eg* to serve liquor, to provide entertainment, music, and so on should not be forgotten when calculating overheads. They can mount up.

WHAT ADVERTISING SHOULD WE DO?

Even hotels in the most prominent positions rarely realise their full potential without some advertising. As it is increasingly expensive, it is of the utmost importance to select your media carefully, consider the content critically and spend your money wisely.

The cheapest source.

Your own guests are your best ambassadors. If looked after properly and sufficiently impressed, they will spread the word and save much formal advertising — and money.

How do you get started?

Until you get known, there are steps you can take to put yourself on the map:

- Introduce yourself at the local Tourist Information Centre. Take a sheaf of brochures and/or business cards.

- Speak to the person who runs the local Hotels Association, which you may already have joined. Be guided by any advice given.

- Call at local places where potential guests stop off, *eg* public houses, cafes, restaurants. Leave a few brochures and/or business cards.

- Send a couple of brochures and several business cards to each of your friends and relatives for them to distribute.

- *Always* carry brochures in the car, ready to hand out.

- Distribute business cards like confetti. Everyone who just might give a lead to business ought to have your card in their pocket.

- Become an active member of the local community. Locals, particularly business people, are there to help you and you them.

- Introduce yourself to other hoteliers nearby. You would like their overflow when they are full and you will then know the best places to pass people when you're full.

- Make sure at least the outside of your hotel is tidy and welcoming.

Existing advertising

You will probably have been pleased to pay for advertising the vendor arranged so that you have a continuing presence in the various guides. The fact that it has been paid for, however, is no guarantee you will derive business from it. It may have become a habit as opposed to being under constant review to assess its financial viability.

Every time someone telephones you with an enquiry, ask where they heard of your hotel and write it down. Keep a permanent record with a view to working out the cost per enquiry at the end of the year. At the same time ruthlessly prune out those sources which are useless.

Assessing your own needs

In journalism, you need to know your market and tailor what you are capable of writing to a specific publication. In the hotel industry, you need to know the type of people who will be attracted to the services you are capable of providing. Once you know this, it will help you accurately assess which publications you should place your advertisements in.

Three guides:

- *Willing's Press Guide*
- *Benn's Media Guide*
- *British Rate and Data* (BRAD)

list virtually all newspaper, magazine and guide book publications, together with circulation figures. They are very expensive to buy but most reference libraries keep them.

Take a good look at specialist interest magazines when there are facilities within easy reach of your hotel. Boating, angling, walking, hill-climbing, pony-trekking, steam railways, nature reserves, are but a few. Remember specialist holiday guides as well.

Once you have listed the publications you think may be suitable, contact them and ask for a media pack. This may well include a copy of the publication, all the advertising information you require and a readership profile. From that profile, you will see what proportion of the various socio-economic categories read that publication.

The standard categories used are:

- A   higher managerial, administrative or professional
- B   intermediate managerial, administrative or professional
- C1   junior managerial, administrative or professional
- C2   skilled manual workers
- D   semi- and unskilled manual workers
- E   those at the lowest level of subsistence.

From all this data, you will be able to ascertain the publications which will reach the maximum number of the type of guest you want to attract, and an appropriate cost.

Weekly local newspapers
Advertisements cost much less in weekly local papers than in their national brothers, are regularly bought by many who habitually visit the area on holiday and, to a lesser extent, by those seeking property (see page 47). Few hoteliers realise this and steer clear of local advertising unless they have a restaurant open to the public. Incidentally, if you know the vendor had a poor reputation, stress 'under new ownership'.

Daily local newspapers
Consider these only when potential guests are already in the area, *eg* business clients, at peak holiday times and/or you are open to non-residents.

The best timing for newspaper and magazine holiday advertisements is not easy to predict. Much depends on the economic climate; if buoyant, holidays get booked up earlier than if the economy is depressed. Certain weeks often work well for particular hotels but no general pattern can be established. Most importantly, don't advertise summer holidays when people's minds are on other things, like Christmas, or autumn breaks when most are taking their main holidays. Check out the timings of newspaper advertisements with regard to:

- Easter breaks
- the main holiday season
- off-season breaks
- Christmas/New Year breaks.

What about content?
An advertisement is not an ego trip for you. It should be a means, in the most economical way possible, of getting across to readers the benefits *to them* of staying at your hotel.

Selling is an art, and advertising is an essential part of your selling process.

Based on well established principles, any advertisement must:

- first grab the reader's *attention*
- stimulate *interest*
- create the *desire*
- prompt *action*.

CASE STUDY

The advertisement (Figure 23), intended for a golfing magazine with predominantly A, B and C1 readers, adheres to the AIDA principle shown above. 'Bourne to be pampered?', using a play on words, is intended to grab the attention of readers who subconsciously think they are of a higher social standing than they actually are. Everyone wants a holiday to remember and, as the attractions unfold, using 'bullet points' for ease of reading, the interest and desire are created. You will notice the Brights set their stall out. In stipulating the age of children, the message is to assure those without children that their tranquillity will not be spoilt by youngsters. Finally, to prompt action, 'immediate' attention is promised, inviting readers to reach for the telephone.

Should you have brochures?

Depending on your circumstances, brochures may form a major part of your advertising campaign. If your hotel photographs well, a colour brochure could justify the high cost involved. Start by asking for two or more quotations, at least one from a specialist company (under Printers in *Yellow Pages*).

A very clear, professional standard photograph is essential for good reproduction. Unless you have the right camera and sufficient expertise, it may be wise to commission a professional photographer. You may wish other shots, *eg* the reception area, the dining room, a bedroom and/or the swimming pool, to be included.

If doing things yourself, remember that people apparently enjoying themselves create a much better image on indoor photographs than an impression that the place is deserted.

Make sure any professional photographer knows *exactly* what you want and quotes in writing, detailing precisely what will be provided.

If going to this sort of expense, it may be worth consulting your local Business Link (see page 61), which can assist, at low cost, with all your marketing needs. A well-devised, professionally prepared marketing

---

BOURNE TO BE PAMPERED?

Make it a holiday to remember at

AA   **THE BOURNE HOTEL**   RAC

* *   **Surfbourne SF91 5QT**   * *

- Quietly situated overlooking beach
- Friendly, relaxing atmosphere
- Attractively-presented high quality food
- Exceptional standard of comfort
- Two golf courses (one championship) nearby
- Well-behaved children over 10 welcome
- Real value for money from £37 pppnt DBB

For *immediate* attention write or phone
Alan or Chris Bright on 01999 121212 *now*.

Fig. 23 How to set out an advertisement.

strategy can pay for itself many times over.

In providing the text for brochures, do not gild the lily to the extent that you contravene the Trades Descriptions Act. Keep brochures to standard paper sizes to avoid unnecessary expense.

Costs and budgeting

Having set an amount you are prepared to spend on advertising, do not exceed it. Easy to say, but not so easy to stick to when bookings are slow coming in. A few years ago at such a time, a hotelier well exceeded his budget by spending £5,000 on a half-page ad in a prestigious newspaper. He got not one reply. By all means build in a little reserve to give your bookings a boost, but don't make such a calamitous mistake yourself.

As well as value for money, always watch out for deadlines. They are often weeks, sometimes months before publication dates.

For an in-depth and absorbing look at advertising, read Michael Bennie's *Do Your Own Advertising* in this series.

CASE STUDY

The Brights have already paid £650 for advertising done by the vendor.

Since newspaper advertising costs from about £50 per single narrow column centimetre, they have opted for two magazines, one a general-interest weekly and one a monthly for golfers. The £500 set aside for February will over four weeks aim at bookings for Easter and summer, the same in May to give a boost for summer, the same near the end of August to publicise autumn breaks and the same in November to advertise Christmas and New Year. The remaining £500 will be for renewing some of their existing advertising, which includes three annual guides, and will depend on the response they get in the current year. As their reputation grows, they will look to reduce this budget substantially.

Invitations to advertise

Sales people will telephone you what will sometimes seem like daily, inviting you to advertise in this or that newspaper, magazine or holiday guide. They are very persuasive and *always* have a special offer or attraction.

Having carefully researched your advertising media, do not be tempted to make a spur-of-the-moment decision. If it sounds attractive, make a note and research the publication but stick to what you have planned. If they are over-persuasive, offer them, instead of a fee, a percentage of the bookings you receive from their advertisements. I have yet to have such an offer accepted!

Widening your horizons

When times are hard, and they can be lean before your reputation has spread, consider what you can offer to generate business.

Speciality weekends, *eg* cooking, painting, photography, guided walks, wine-tasting, creative writing and so on are much in vogue. Is there any sort of weekend you could run yourself, or maybe organise with a guest host?

Other ways of generating turnover in quiet times are to:

- do cream teas (providing you are in the right location)
- be host to local organisations for lunches, dinners, meetings and the like
- host small conferences for companies
- run whist drives, chess and/or bridge evenings.

A 'conference pack' showing what is needed is available free of charge from your regional Tourist Board.

Ask yourself:

- What special knowledge have I got?
- What facilities can I offer?
- Who can I offer them to?

Make sure, however, you don't contravene the law. If your liquor licence is purely residential, under no circumstances can you serve alcohol to outside groups. If you organise any music for dancing, you many need an entertainment licence from the local authority (this does not apply in Scotland if you already hold a liquor licence).

CHECKLIST

Do you know:

- How to fix your tariff?
- How to price your bar goods?
- How VAT affects your prices?
- All about holiday insurance?
- How to get the bills settled?
- What banking is costing you?
- What a trade association can do for you?
- How your rates bills are assessed?
- How to publicise your new hotel?
- What are the best publications for your advertisements?
- How to word an advertisement?
- How you could increase your turnover?

9

Up and Running

SETTING THE TONE

'What a lovely place, it'll do us just fine,' 'Not up to our usual standard' and 'Far too posh for us' are all remarks that could be made about the same hotel. Everyone is different and every hotelier will be aiming at a certain type of client. It is up to you to set the tone for the sort of guest *you* want to attract, in every department of your hotel.

The exterior image

Flaking paint, dirty walls, dingy windows, drab curtains and an unkempt garden will deter all but the most desperate guest. The outside is seen as a reflection of what can be expected on the inside.

The image inside

Unless yours is the only hotel in the area, or the only one with vacancies, those who knock at your door are presumably reasonably happy with what they have seen from the outside.

The reception area, be it a proper desk with all the trimmings or just a hallway, is the next hurdle you have to get guests over. If it is scruffy, dimly-lit or smells, don't be surprised when those who had intended to contribute to your livelihood make some excuse and disappear. If either the outside or the reception area is anything less than you would like to see yourself when looking for accommodation, do something about it before you go bust.

The welcome

'From the moment we met, we felt so at home' is the best compliment any guest can pay you. It means you have got your welcome right. When staying in a strange place, guests need to feel comfortable from the earliest possible moment.

When you first arrive at a hotel, especially after a long journey, would **you** like to be offered a cup of tea on the house by a friendly host? Of course you would.

If guests have brought in their luggage, take it or get it taken straight to their room. If not, and especially if they have parked on a yellow line, get the cases from their car and set their minds at rest by directing them where to park.

Next, escort your guests into a comfortable lounge area while someone assisting you prepares their complimentary tray. Introduce yourself, including your first name. Guests will then have the option whether to use your first name and to offer their own. Introduce the newcomers to any other guests who are around.

Once you are sitting down with them and pleasantries about their journey and the weather have been dispensed with, you have the opportunity to find out any likes or dislikes they have, especially in the food line, and particularly if you serve a set menu. You will also be able to take orders for newspapers, if required. If they are staying more than just overnight, consider loaning them a front door key so they can come and go as they wish. Let them know subtly how you run your hotel including any house rules that might apply to them.

Registration
By the **Immigration (Hotel Records) Order 1972, as amended**, before the guests leave you to go to their room you should ask them to **register**. Anyone over 16 must provide their full name and nationality. In the case of aliens, the number and place of issue of their passport should be added. On leaving, aliens must show their next destination. Concessions are likely to be made in the legislation for members of the European Union. Such records have to be kept for 12 months and be open for inspection by police.

It is when registering that you will find it convenient to mention payment of the final bill, assuming you have decided this to be your policy (see pages 135–136).

Orienting your guests
Finally, make sure your guests know where everything is: the dining room, the bar, toilets, the fire escape, and draw their attention to the notices setting out what they should do in case of fire. Wish them a pleasant stay and assure them you can help with information about local shops, beauty spots, walks and so on.

Within half an hour of arriving, they should be glad they chose your hotel, feel completely at home and be sufficiently impressed to be thinking about returning.

Although you may feel justified in modifying your procedure if your guests are mainly overnight B & B, they still need to be impressed if they are to return.

WHAT SHOULD OUR HOUSE RULES BE?

No matter how free and easy you may want to be in running your hotel, your likes and dislikes will be reflected in any rules you make, whether written or unwritten. Have you stayed in a hotel where the owners pride themselves in having no rules? It's absolute chaos! Whatever you decide, stick to it so everyone knows where they stand.

Accepting children

Well-behaved children can bring a lot of pleasure to guests outside the family, ill-behaved ones a lot of displeasure, even misery. Nobody wants to be disturbed in the middle of the night by a baby screaming its head off, or to be woken up at some unearthly hour by children racing around. And no hotelier wants kids wiping their greasy hands on the posh new curtains after a meal.

- The answer is, know your clientele.

If yours is a family hotel, the odd unruly group will have to be put up with, you will have furnished the place sensibly, bearing in mind the abuse to which it may be subjected, and you will be geared up to serve the sort of food youngsters prefer. You may also need to serve food for young children earlier than the adults' mealtimes.

If, on the other hand, you cater mainly for couples, many of whom may be well past their first flush of youth, set a minimum age for children and keep to it. Just one early morning bout of knock-down-ginger could lose you a lot of future business.

Should you take only the occasional family group on holiday, it is not a good idea to have two or more staying at the same time. Kids tend to side with a new friend against their own brothers or sisters and friction which affects the other guests can result.

Accepting pets

As there are good and bad parents, so there are good and bad dog owners. Those who bring a bed for a clean, properly house-trained dog, which they leave in the car while they eat and take for walks well away from the hotel, present no problems. Those who leave an anxious pet to roam around their bedroom while they take meals or whatever and then let it use your garden as a loo, can cause you all sorts of problems.

To cater for the inconsiderate dog owner, it is advisable to draw up a list of rules if you accept pets and send it with your brochure when you receive an enquiry about taking dogs, together with a notification of any charge you make. Most dogs shed some hairs which stick like glue to carpets. This means that cleaning a room which has had a dog in it takes longer than normal and it is reasonable for a small charge to reflect this.

It is best not to include food in your terms for dogs, as it will probably be different to what the dog is used to and could upset its digestion and what follows, with disastrous results. Leave the owner to give it what it's used to.

Consider the following for inclusion in your list of conditions:

- dogs must not be left unattended in the bedroom
- no pets may be allowed on any furniture
- dogs must be on a lead while being led through the hotel
- no dog may be allowed to foul the hotel garden
- dogs are not allowed in the dining room (and wherever else)
- owners will be responsible for all damage, however caused.

The responsible owner will accept all reasonable conditions. Should a booking not result after you have sent your list of rules, console yourself that the owner knows the dog better than you do!

Always set out your stall when offering accommodation. If you accept pets subject to certain conditions, say so in your brochure. It is better for a guest with an allergy or a phobia to know you accept pets before booking rather than to find out after arrival.

Many guests always take their dogs with them on holiday. For such people, Farm Holiday Guide Publications Ltd of Abbey Mill Business Centre, Paisley PA1 1TJ (Tel: (0141) 887 0428) publish an annual guide to accommodation where pets are accepted, entitled *Pets Welcome!*

Smoking

An emotive subject? If you smoke, you may not have considered the issue from the point of view of non-smokers. However, those who choose not to smoke often regard the smell of stale tobacco with distaste. In addition, the smell gets into bed linen, wall coverings and curtains and will invade the nostrils of non-smokers literally for days after a heavy smoker has left. Some of your guests, probably a majority, will not smoke and need to be considered.

A partial ban, *eg* in the dining room and/or bedrooms, will work most of the time. Some, however, will flout the rules and in the absence of ashtrays in no-smoking areas will use a cup, plate, saucer, litter bin and/or throw cigarette ends out of the window.

Again, it is important to know your guests. If a good proportion don't smoke, at least have some no-smoking bedrooms and a sitting area where non-smokers can go without having to breathe fouled air. If guests' visits are marred because they can't get away from the smell of smoke, they will not return. Some hoteliers have found their bookings soar as a result of banning smoking altogether — and publicising the fact.

Notices

Enough notices are required by law to be displayed without adding any of your own unnecessarily. Those already mentioned, not all of which may apply to your hotel, are:

- tariff for hotel residents
- tariff for non-resident restaurant users
- hotelier's liability — Hotel Proprietors Act
- hotelier's liability towards employees
- notification under Business Names Act
- what to do in case of fire — guests' bedrooms
- what to do in case of fire — fire call points
- what to do in case of fire — staff quarters
- bar — Weights and Measures Act
- bar — price list
- Health and Safety at Work, *etc* Act (if each employee has not been handed a leaflet).

A surfeit of other notices, like 'please don't bang this door', 'don't run down the stairs', 'keep off the banister', or 'please clean the bath after use' can be a source of ridicule. You will need, however, to put a 'private' sign on all doors where guests are not admitted. If not, someone will wander into your bedroom, lounge or whatever, sooner or later.

Notifying guests

Many of your rules will have been set out in your brochure and tariff, *eg* ages of children, acceptance of pets and so on. If you have set rules with regard to payment of balances due on bookings, tell your guests when you send confirmations.

A complete **booking confirmation** on which you will insert and/or delete words as appropriate and setting out a few suggestions on settlement of balances is shown in Figure 24. Directions to help guests find your hotel set out on the back of the confirmation should ensure that guests bring the form with them, thus avoiding any dispute. Copies

THE BOURNE HOTEL

Mr. B. Discerning   1 May 200X
33 London Road
London W6

BOOKING CONFIRMATION

We acknowledge receipt of your booking for **TWO** persons in **ONE** double room with en suite bathroom and sea view from **15th August 200X** to **22nd August 200X** to include dinner, bed and breakfast.

Total cost, including VAT @ $17^1/2\%$, **£476.28** less deposit **£50.00** (Invoice No. **072** enclosed) Balance **£426.28**
You may pay your balance

(a) In cash or by Mastercard or Visa at any time before departure;
(b) By cheque subject to the following conditions:
A cheque is accepted on day of departure only if covered by a cheque guarantee card for the whole amount.
Otherwise a signed cheque must be deposited with the proprietor on arrival or, at the latest, four days before departure for clearance.

SHOULD YOU PAY THE BALANCE TO ARRIVE WITH US BY **15th July** YOUR BALANCE WILL BE REDUCED TO **415.62.**

Hotel Insurance

We rely upon the hotel business for our living and whereas we do not expect you to be able to afford to pay for a holiday you are unable to take, neither can we afford the loss that your failure to take up a booking may cause us.

If you were forced to cancel your holiday, we would of course make every effort to relet your room/s but, should we not succeed, we reserve the right to levy cancellation charges and in any event you would lose your deposit.

We regard hotel insurance so important that, providing you complete and send off the enclosed proposal form and premium, whether or not you opt for wider cover, we will deduct from your bill the cancellation premium which amounts to £10.00. This will also safeguard your deposit.

Resident Proprietors: Andrew and Christine Bright
VAT No. 121 2121 21

Fig. 24. Booking confirmation letter.

should be filed with your invoices.

Instead of notices all over the place which quickly become soiled, any other requests you may wish to make to your guests are best communicated in a folder in the bedroom. Start your personal message with, for example, Andrew and Christine Bright welcome you to the Bourne Hotel and wish you a pleasant stay. For your comfort and convenience, may we point out the following:

- Times of meals . . .
- We would appreciate it if wet outdoor clothing were not brought into the bedroom. If handed to us, we will be pleased to dry it for you, free of charge.
- Please be so kind as not to remove towels from your bathroom. We will do our best to find you one for beach use on request.
- Should you require any additional bed linen, pillows, *etc* please do not hesitate to ask.

After any other requests and information, you could end: 'Thank you for coming to see us at The Bourne. We hope you will visit us again.'

Most guests respond to requests made in a courteous manner. To add to the welcome and enhance the personal touch, a bunch of flowers, a small packet of fudge or box of chocolates with the hotel name on it, or maybe a complimentary ballpen with the hotel name and telephone number (many items can be personalised without huge outlay) will do your reputation no harm at all. Result: more bookings, less formal advertising, more profit.

WHICH FACILITIES SHOULD BE OFFERED?

Any facilities or services offered must always be considered in terms of the type of establishment you are running and, if appropriate, staffing levels.

All-day service

In a small hotel, the extra cost of having staff on hand all day would not be justified unless (a) you open to non-residents and (b) a definite need exists.

Use of garden

If you have a pleasant, reasonably large garden, by all means allow your guests to use it, especially if it contains a swimming pool (don't forget to assess the risks). Do, however, try to keep a secluded spot partitioned off for your own use. You will come to value your free time highly and will need to relax away from your guests.

Facilities for non-residents

Once you open to non-residents, it is in your interests to ensure it's not to the detriment of your residents. Some guests even pick 'their own' parking spot when staying a week and any intrusion by 'outsiders' is frowned upon. If that guest then cannot get service at the bar, or has to wait while you see to non-residents, you are well on your way to losing a client.

Many hoteliers open to non-residents have a much faster turnover of guests than their 'residents-only' counterparts, precisely for the reason mentioned above. Large hotels are, by their nature, impersonal. If your small one goes the same way, your resident guests will not be impressed.

Newspapers

Whether staying on business or for pleasure, many guests like a morning paper. It is a service you ought to offer if you already have a newspaper delivered. The mark-up on newspapers is high and if there is competition in the area, negotiate a year-round discount of, say, ten per cent.

Beverages

In small establishments, room service is a bind. It takes up far too much time for too little profit. The provision of the wherewithal to make tea and coffee when the guest wants it is of benefit to all.

Sachets of tea, coffee and sugar, and tiny jugs of milk and cream are readily available in bulk from the 'cash and carry'. Should you, though, put in a fresh supply every day free of charge? If you do, some will put what they don't use in their suitcase on the principle they have paid for it. A way of stopping that mean practice and helping a local charity is, after the initial supply, to sell the sachets, *etc* at the nearest penny above cost to you and put the proceeds in the charity tin. The scheme can be outlined in your 'welcome' folder. Very few guests will protest.

Disabled guests

If your hotel has ground-floor bedrooms (or a lift) you may consider taking disabled guests. The minimum requirements are listed in the ETC leaflet *The National Accessible Scheme* (see Appendix).

FOOD AND DRINK

Buying food in

Particularly in the early stages, it is very easy to chase around getting various food products from the places you feel give you best value for money. Don't! It is right you should want to do the best by your guests, but your objectives can be achieved without spending all your precious free time going from supplier to supplier. To be able to look after your guests properly, without making mistakes because of fatigue, you need some time for relaxation.

Make a weekly or fortnightly visit to the wholesale cash and carry. If you can't get all you want there, invite a few suppliers to quote, or speak to your new friends in the Association and find out who delivers the best.

'Delivers' is the key word. Meat and fish products can, if required, be supplied 'portion controlled' to your specification. If anything substandard is delivered, send it straight back and require an immediate replacement. After a *very* short time, you may be known as 'that awkward . . .' but you will get exactly what you want.

Choice of menu

It is impossible to provide a wide choice of freshly prepared dishes without enormous wastage, meaning you have to charge astronomical prices. Twenty guests *do* sometimes all ask for the same main course.

Without wastage, a large choice of dishes has to be supplied from the freezer and defrosted, taking but a matter of minutes with a good commercial microwave oven. Since many restaurants use the same supplier of frozen foods, it is possible to recognise the 'duck à l'orange', the 'chicken supreme' and so on in a number of places. Although such food is often prepared by chefs and is of good quality, it can also be prepared in your kitchen and frozen for future use.

You could fall in line with several prestigious restaurants which provide just one, freshly cooked main course per day, an alternative being served only with prior notice. With this system, everyone gains. Less wastage and fewer staff for the hotel; tastier, healthier food for the customer.

Alternative dishes

What happens, though, if a guest is allergic to your *carte du jour*? This is where the frozen alternative comes into its own. Many dishes supplied by frozen food companies, *eg* the ubiquitous 'duck à l'orange', come as 'boil-in-the-bag'. Dropped into a pan of boiling water, it is ready to serve in 20 minutes and is very useful to have as a stand-by. (It has been known for restaurants to use nothing but 'boil-in-the-bag' food!)

Staggered mealtimes

To provide properly cooked food at different times takes a lot of time and trouble. Some restaurants stake their reputation on taking such pains. In others, it often means food which has been kept hot, sometimes for long periods, or warmed up. It is much easier for the cook, who can ensure for example that vegetables retain their 'nuttiness', if meals are cooked ready to be served at a specific time. Much depends on what your clientele expects.

In the dining room

Cutlery and crockery

It is no good creating the right atmosphere with subtle background music, soft lighting and crisp tablecloths if the cutlery and crockery are poor quality. Use the best available commensurate with the standards you have set for your hotel. If you have a dishwasher, make sure everything you buy is 'dishwasher-safe'.

Serviettes

Paper or linen? What would *you* expect in a hotel like yours? Good-quality paper ones are available and are infinitely preferable to putting out a linen one that has been used before. Guests might ask themselves, by whom? Is this the one I used last night? Have they got them mixed up?

A compromise is to use a fresh linen one each day for dinner and a paper one at breakfast. Laundry and replacement are costs that have to be considered if linen ones are used.

Metal pots

Providing they are kept clean and shiny, metal pots for tea, coffee, hot water and milk are by far the most practical. They don't chip, nor do they crack if you put boiling water into a cold one. Unless pottery is an essential part of the scene in your hotel, stay with metal pots.

Pre-packed goods

'Messy' is a word that immediately comes to mind with the wide range of products available in individual portions. They always seem difficult to open, particularly for elderly guests, and with preserves and butter it's difficult to avoid getting sticky fingers. The advantage, of course, is that it saves a lot of preparation time. Use the minimum you find necessary.

Providing wine

If you hold a liquor licence, wine can be sold only in specific quantities: 25cl, 50cl, 75cl or 1 litre. If by the glass, the measures have to be: 125ml, 175ml or in multiples thereof. Wine lists will need to show the quantities, also wine glasses and carafes must have a line showing the relevant measure. There is no longer a legal requirement to show the alcoholic strength.

Although it can be fun compiling a wine list, especially the tasting . . . (so you can describe the wine accurately!), the amount you need to invest might be unjustified in a small hotel. The *Which? Wine Guide* will help you put the subject into perspective, give you ideas which wine to keep and show you how to describe it.

Since it is air coming into contact with the wine that causes deterioration, once a bottle has been opened any that is unused will quickly become undrinkable unless a closure method, now widely available, is used to expel air from the void area. Wine boxes overcome this problem since the aluminium container in the box collapses as wine is drawn off, so keeping the air out.

The range available has improved enormously in recent years. Try keeping two or three whites in the fridge as your house wine ready to serve by the glass, half carafe or carafe, bearing in mind the legal quantities. There is never a need to serve dreadful plonk as house wine, yet many hoteliers do.

Price the quantities competitively to encourage the bargain hunter. As a guide, start with a bottle or carafe and double what you paid for it. For example, from a 3-litre box costing £12, a one-litre carafe (8 x 125ml glasses) could be priced at £8, a half-litre at £4.50 and each 125ml glass at £1.25.

If you don't hold a liquor licence, you may allow guests to provide their own wine. Be prepared for requests to chill it and to provide glasses (which need washing up).

Smoking

Irrespective of any other rules about smoking, it is reasonable not to allow it where other guests' enjoyment of the food you have gone to so much trouble to provide may be spoilt. Whether this means a total ban in the dining room or the provision of 'no-smoking' tables depends on your circumstances and the space available.

How do you run a bar?

The legal requirements
These are set out in Schedule 2 to the **Licensing Act 1964, as amended,**

and the **Licensing (Scotland) Act 1976**. New applicants need to serve
notice at least 21 days before the court hearing on:

- the Clerk to the Licensing Justices
- the Police
- the Fire Brigade
- the Local Authority
- the clerk to the Parish Council (rural areas only).

How to run it

Running a small hotel bar, you will almost certainly not be tied to a
brewery, meaning you are free to buy your supplies from the cheapest
source available and to take advantage of special offers.

Beer in casks and bottles may be obtained from a licensed trade
wholesaler who will loan you any necessary equipment.

Depending on circumstances, think carefully before serving beer
on draught. It has a very limited life, needs to be served cooled and
the beer pipes must be cleaned through at least once a week.
Wastage results. Dregs in glasses, which are the result of dirty beer
pipes (let no one tell you different), are unacceptable. However, if
you have the necessary quick turnover, draught beer at a reasonable
price is what may keep guests in your bar.

In spite of decimalisation, the UK pint (.57 of a litre) looks safe at the
moment. Optics, however, can be only 25ml, 35ml or multiples thereof
and the customer must be able to see the top of the liquid in the optic.

Intoxicating liquor may be served to *residents* 24 hours a day.
Otherwise the hours are usually 11am to 11pm Monday to Saturday, 12
noon to 10.30pm on Sundays, all plus one hour 'supper hour' extension
in licensed restaurants and a further half-hour drinking-up time.

You will see by the **Residential Licence** in Figure 25 that you need
to provide a public room, other than the dining room, in which alcohol
may not be consumed. In smaller establishments this may mean your
lounge will have to be a 'non-drink' area. Further, as can be seen in the
conditions, beverages other than intoxicating liquor must be made available as an ancillary to a meal. The two types of licence may be issued as
a joint **Residential and Restaurant Licence**.

Instead, you could apply for a **Full On Licence with conditions**,
otherwise known as a **Functions Licence**. Though the conditions are
largely the same as for a **Residential and Restaurant Licence**, an extra
condition allows the licensee to serve intoxicating liquor to persons
attending bona fide functions at premises where bona fide meals are
served, such functions being organised by an individual or organisation

SPECIMEN

RESIDENTIAL LICENCE

AT the Licensing Sessions holden at the Court House, <ADDRESS_OF_COURT> on the <DOH> for the Licensing District of <DIVISION>

THE Licensing Justices for the said District grant unto

<NAMES>

This Justices' Licence authorising <HIM_HER_THEM> to sell by retail at the licensed premises known as

<PREMISES>

<TYPE_OF_LIQUOR> for consumption <ON_OR_OFF> the premises, in accordance with the conditions endorsed hereon.

THE owner(s) of the premises in respect of which this licence is granted is/are

<OWNERS>

THIS licence is granted subject to the conditions endorsed hereon and shall be in force from this day, until the Fourth day of April, 2001.

GIVEN under the official Seal of the Licensing Justices which is hereto afixed under their authority by me

Clerk to the Justices

CONDITIONS

1. Intoxicating liquor shall not be sold or supplied on the premises otherwise than to persons residing there or their private friends bona fide entertained by them at their own expense and for consumption by such persons or their private friends so entertained by them on the premises or with a meal supplied at but to be consumed off the premises.

2. Suitable beverages other than intoxicating liquor shall be equally available for consumption with or otherwise as an ancillary to meals served in the licensed premises.

3. There shall be afforded in the premises for persons provided with board and lodging for reward, adequate sitting accommodation in a room not used or to be used for sleeping accommodation for the service of substantial refreshment or for the supply or consumption of intoxicating liquor.

Fig. 25. A residential licence.

SPECIMEN

RESIDENTIAL AND RESTAURANT LICENCE

AT the Licensing Sessions holden at the Court House, <ADDRESS_OF_COURT> on the <DOH> for the Licensing District of <DIVISION>

THE Licensing Justices for the said District grant unto

<NAMES>

This Justices' Licence authorising <HIM_HER_THEM> to sell by retail at the licensed premises known as

<PREMISES>

<TYPE_OF_LIQUOR> for consumption <ON_OR_OFF> the premises, in accordance with the conditions endorsed hereon.

THE owner(s) of the premises in respect of which this licence is granted is/are

<OWNERS>

THIS licence is granted subject to the conditions endorsed hereon and shall be in force from this day, until the Fourth day of April, 2001.

GIVEN under the official Seal of the Licensing Justices which is hereto afixed under their authority by me

Clerk to the Justices

RESIDENTIAL AND RESTAURANT LICENCE CONDITIONS

1. Intoxicating liquor shall not be sold or supplied on the premises otherwise than:

a) to persons taking table meals there and for consumption by such a person as an ancillary to his meal, or

b) to persons residing there or their private friends bona fide entertained by them at their own expense and for consumption by such persons or their private friends so entertained by them on the premises or with a meal supplied at but to be consumed off the premises.

2. Suitable beverages other than intoxicating liquor shall be equally available for consumption with or otherwise as an ancillary to meals served in the licensed premises.

3. There shall be afforded in the premises for persons provided with board and lodging for reward, adequate sitting accommodation in a room not used or to be used for sleeping accommodation for the service of substantial refreshment or for the supply or consumption of intoxicating liquor.

Fig. 26. A restaurant licence.

SPECIMEN

**GRANT OF
JUSTICES' LICENCE**

AT the Licensing Sessions holden at the Court House, <ADDRESS_OF_COURT> on the <DOH> for the Licensing District of <DIVISION>

THE Licensing Justices for the said District grant unto

<NAMES>

This Justices' Licence authorising <HIM_HER_THEM> to sell by retail at the premises known as

<PREMISES>

<TYPE_OF_LIQUOR> for consumption <ON_OR_OFF> the premises.

THE owner(s) of the premises in respect of which this licence is granted is/are

<OWNERS>

THIS licence is granted subject to the conditions endorsed hereon and shall be in force from this day, until the Fourth day of April, 2001.

GIVEN under the official Seal of the Licensing Justices which is hereto afixed under their authority by me

Clerk to the Licensing Justices

CONDITIONS

1. Intoxicating liquor shall not be sold or supplied on the premises otherwise than to:

a) Persons taking table meals there and for consumption by such a person as an ancillary to his meal, and

b) Persons residing there or their private friends bona fide entertained by them at their own expense and for consumption by such a person or his private friends so entertained by him either on the premises, or with a meal supplied at but to be consumed off the premises.

c) Persons attending bona fide functions held at the premises at which bona fide meals are served, such functions being organised by an individual or organisation hiring the premises for the period.

2. Suitable beverages other than intoxicating liquor (including drinking water) shall be equally available for consumption with or otherwise as an ancillary to meals served on the premises.

3. There shall be afforded in the premises for persons provided with board and lodging for reward, adequate sitting accommodation in a room not used or to be used for sleeping accommodation, for the service of substantial refreshment or for the supply or consumption of intoxicating liquor.

Fig. 27. A functions licence.

hiring the premises for the period.

The subtle distinction is that persons attending the function and using the bar, unless specified, do not need to drink only as ancillary to a meal and may not, depending on the wording of the conditions, even have to have a sit-down meal.

Children's Certificates

In the circumstances outlined above, or if your bar is open to non-residents, you may want to be able to legally allow children under 14 in your bar (as opposed to a room set aside). Children under 14 are otherwise allowed to be there only if they are *your* children, or resident, or passing through to another part of the premises. To be allowed by law to have 'outsiders' under 14 in your bar (they must always be accompanied by an adult), apply to the Licensing Justices for a **Children's Certificate**.

DEALING WITH ENQUIRIES

Attitude

Whether it is in person, on the telephone or by letter, first impressions count. How you communicate could make the difference between the success and failure of your business.

Always appear presentable, cheerful and helpful when answering the door. Answer your telephone with a greeting such as 'The Bourne Hotel, good morning, how can I help you?' Immediately the right impression is given, your courtesy and desire to help are apparent. Potential guests will feel you care and will respond favourably.

There are still far too many hoteliers who adopt an uncaring and rude approach. Don't be one of them, even if you have had a rough day. As with day-to-day dealings with guests, never let your problems become theirs. Insist on your staff adopting the same attitude as you do.

Answerphone

Since it is unlikely you will have a receptionist always on duty, an answerphone can cover times you cannot answer the telephone personally. Any answer is better than none at all — and a booking may result. But the message must be right. Don't let your potential guests be put off by the sort of dreadful recorded message you often hear.

There will always be those who put the receiver down the moment they hear a recorded message start, often because they can't bring themselves to talk to a machine. Show such people you recognise the problem and you just may stop them ringing the next hotelier on their list.

Whatever you do, don't record a message that is cold, impersonal or gives the impression you have one foot in the grave. And make sure your answerphone picks up calls promptly and delivers your message clearly and accurately with nothing cut off the beginning or the end.

Case study

Andrew Bright, using a lively voice, recorded the following message for the Bourne Hotel answerphone.

'Hello. Of course you don't like talking to a machine. Nor do I! But we can't always be free to answer calls in person, so please don't hang up. This is Andrew Bright of the Bourne Hotel, Surfbourne, and if you would like to leave a message please do so. If not, just say your name and phone number after the tone signal and we will call you back as soon as we can. Thank you for calling us.' (Bleep.)

Requests for brochures/details

Make sure that *every* request for information is dealt with straight away, especially if you rely to a large extent on advertising through brochures. Send them out with a first class stamp by the next post, even if you have to hot-foot it down to the postbox.

People often request brochures from a few hotels the same day. Make sure yours is the first to arrive. In your haste, however, avoid the use of 'with compliments' slips. They smack of impersonality. Just a short letter, thanking the client for their enquiry and inviting further contact if they have any queries, is all that is required.

Many people feel that if a simple request for a brochure cannot be dealt with promptly, the hotelier doesn't care whether a booking is made or not. You need to be seen to care.

Taking bookings

A chart is absolutely essential for entering records of bookings. Get a system set up from the outset. Use either A4 or A3 (double A4 size) sheets, one for each month, and fix them into a folder. It will not always be convenient to go to the same spot to check a chart that is stuck to the wall.

The moment a booking is made, use other sheets at the front of the folder and take a note of:

- the date and time
- the person's name, address and telephone number
- how they heard of you
- the dates of the booking (as verified on your chart)
- the number of persons

ENTRY NO.	DATE	TIME	NAME	ADDRESS/TELE NO.	SOURCE	DATES FROM	TO.	No. of PERSONS	ROOM No.	INV. DEP. DATE	REMARKS
1/99	3/1	11am	Mr. C.R. MARCHANT	53 CHEYNE VILLAS, LONDON RD, READING RG993CV 0118 999111	AA	7/1	21/1	2	2	042 £90 8/1	DB+B Small dog 'Dany'
2/99	4/1	7pm	Mrs. M. SMYTHE	2 FOREST VIEW, LONDON ES 2JT, No phone	Tourist Board	14/1	19/1	2	3	040 £35 5/1	DB+B with friend Mr. R. JAMES
3/99	4/1	7.15pm	Mr. K. WILSON	1169 Harbor Lane, WATFORD WD64 2HL 01923 777277	FHG.	21/1	28/1	3	1/5	041 £54 7/1	BB only (exc. 2 '/2?) 2 Wards mother in 5
4/99											
5/99											

Fig. 28. Entries from a booking chart.

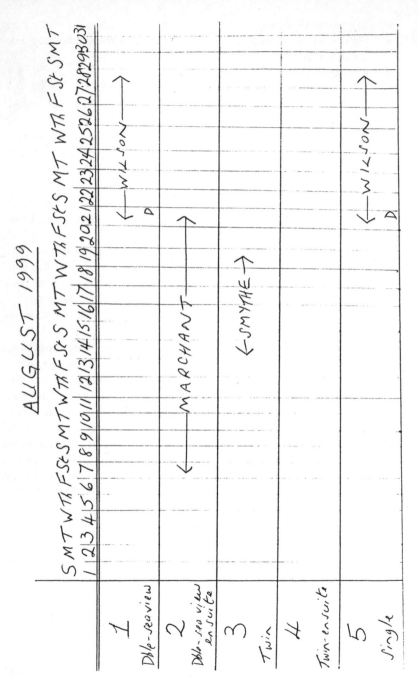

Fig. 29. Monthly booking chart.

- the rooms allocated
- the deposit required (leaving space for the invoice number and date it is received)
- any relevant remarks or requests.

As you confirm the dates and the accommodation you have allocated, enter the name on your booking chart *in pencil*, clearly marking the nights of stay and the meal arrangements. As soon as the deposit is received, make out an invoice (see page 121), enter the number and date on your booking form and ink in the name on the chart. (People do change their minds, especially before a deposit is sent.)

Account for the cash received, make out a confirmation and send it to the client with a short covering letter wishing them a safe journey and looking forward to meeting them.

Finally transfer the name, address, telephone number and dates into your A4 indexed book (see page 83) together with your entry number. As well as being your permanent entry for making remarks about your guests' special fads, it will serve as an index for the year's bookings.

Typical entries in your booking chart folder could look like those in Figures 28 and 29. It may at first glance seem like a lot of work but it takes only a few minutes, especially since your booking confirmations will be pre-printed and you will have a proper record second to none.

No hard and fast rule can be laid down about whether or not you should take only complete weekly bookings, say, Saturday to Saturday. In some resorts, virtually every hotelier sticks to this format, particularly in the main summer season. You will have to be guided by what is the norm for your location and what the demand is. It will be difficult to get it right all the time but bear in mind that taking a Sunday to Sunday booking in the main season could leave a room or, worse still, rooms vacant for the first Saturday night and for the Sunday to Friday of the following week.

Telephone sales enquiries

Almost as often as you get calls inviting you to advertise, you will get those trying to make appointments for reps to call and try to sell you new kitchens, double glazing and so on. The time wasted on these calls could be losing you bookings. Cut them off.

Staying sane

How to deal with complaints

'But if I work hard at impressing my guests, I won't get complaints, will I?' Unfortunately you will. 'There's always one', as the saying goes.

When you work extremely hard at trying to impress everyone, it is very upsetting to get a complaint.

Never be other than courteous, no matter how unjustified you think it may be. But don't make out you're in the wrong if you believe the opposite. 'I'm sorry you felt obliged to complain', or 'I'm sorry if our choice of . . . was not to your liking', is as far as you should go. Unfortunately, some guests take a delight in complaining and if they find you are a pushover, your life won't be worth living.

On the other hand, if you or any of your staff are in the wrong, admit it. If it helps smooth things over, give what concession you can. Never use staff as a scapegoat because what employees do is down to you. (Ask yourself if you've trained them correctly.)

Don't forget to make a note in your record book of professional complainers. You might find you're full next time they want to make a booking!

Know the law and comply with it
Your guests will come from many walks of life. The chances are you won't know when a policeman, or tax inspector, or customs officer, or. . . stays with you. A few in that type of occupation take a sadistic pleasure in informing on others, and if you continually flout the law sooner or later you will get an unwelcome visitor who could be instrumental in putting you out of business.

Keep up to date with the law as it affects you, comply with it and don't fear the knock on the door.

Don't take on more than you can cope with
If you become stressed, no one will benefit. Ill health will catch up with you sooner or later. Of course you should concern yourself about your guests and how your business is going, but if to comply with a request will worry you, say 'no'. Everyone has limitations. Know yours.

HOW DO WE STAY AHEAD OF THE COMPETITION?

Assess your competitors

An inspection of the exteriors of your neighbouring competitors' hotels will soon tell you if the outside of your own is up to scratch. It should be at least as good as, preferably better than, the others. Remember AIDA, the principles of selling (see pages 141–2). Unless your hotel creates the 'attraction', you have fallen at the first hurdle.

Study your competitors' advertisements. Do they give you any ideas?

Is there anything in them that ought to be in your ads? Are they advertising anything that you ought to be doing? Would dinner by candlelight go down well in your hotel, for example?

From time to time and without any prompting, your guests will tell you about other hotels they have stayed at, the way they do things, good as well as bad. Sometimes you may think them indiscreet and wonder what they will tell others about yours. At least take notice of what is said. Feed off others' ideas — it may help you boost your business.

Never fear the big hotels, nor the cheapie B and B. They are, or should be, in different leagues.

Be different

The occasional 'way-out' hotel rarely flourishes, so don't be bizarre, just different. Be the best of your type of hotel.

If your food is exceptional, make a meal of it in your advertisements. If you make a point of presenting the food attractively, say so; food is first 'tasted' with the eyes. Proclaim, if it is so, the fact your food is freshly cooked using local produce. Then make sure it lives up to what you've said about it when you put it on the plate. (Incidentally, in most cases oval plates allow you to present food to best advantage.)

'Comfort' is another key word. Hotel beds generally are dreadfully uncomfortable. A large proportion of the population suffers from back pain. If it is made worse by the fact that your beds sag in the middle, repeat bookings will not result. Back sufferers who find your beds give them proper support and allow them to sleep well will be only too pleased to return, if only to be guaranteed a good night's sleep.

Provide the best quality beds you can and don't keep the fact to yourself. You will then rank among the small minority who give this subject proper consideration.

By keeping a record of all guests in your index book, you are already exceptional. Among the data will be any birthdays, anniversaries and the like that come to your notice. Whether you bake a little cake, give a small box of chocolates, or recognise the occasion in another way, you will be providing that extra touch. Things such as a small gift in the bedroom on arrival, flowers on the table, individual name tags for serviette holders, make guests feel they are other than a commodity.

If you want to be really different, designate your bedrooms according to the colour scheme, or in line with the flower depicted on the wallpaper. It might be 'Bedroom 1' to you, but guests could know it as 'the pink room,' or 'the honeysuckle room'. Use your own imagination to create the sort of experience for your guests that they will want to repeat.

168 Buying & Running a Small Hotel

Be professional

Without going over the top, make sure you always appear tidily dressed in front of your guests. A good appearance combined with a professional, caring attitude will earn you the respect of others. When you know what you're doing, it shows.

Be friendly

Surveys of hotels without exception level criticism at a large number of hoteliers for being miserable, even surly. You may ask what they are doing in the business since guests don't go back for a second dose of doom and gloom.

You will not always feel like being friendly but your livelihood depends on it. Hoteliers who have to maintain a high advertising budget suffer in leaner times much more than those who build up a happy family of regular guests.

How do we stay profitable?

Charging

Would you object to paying for a glass of tap water? Some hoteliers make a charge to cover the wear and tear on glasses and the washing up. Most, thankfully, regard it as being mean.

How about filling a thermos flask with boiling water? If no charge is made, who pays for the electricity?

You will deduce there is a fine line between what it is acceptable to charge for and that which should be complimentary. If *you* would expect to pay for a service, make a charge. If it is borderline, a small donation in the hospice tin might be appropriate.

Keep tariffs realistic

Keep tariffs at a level that provides you with a sensible profit. As costs go up, so will your guests' incomes. No matter how much you may enjoy your new lifestyle, do not undercharge. Increased costs to you must be reflected in higher tariffs. At the same time, giving value for money is essential.

Pursue losses

If you do not insist on payment of debts, it is unfair on the guests who pay and who will have to share the burden that debtors cause. If your procedures for settlement of balances are tight enough, you will not be owed money from that quarter. Losses caused through bookings not taken up are less easy to control.

Once someone has made a booking, they have entered into a legally enforceable contract. If they do not turn up or contact you and you lose money as a result, it is right for you to pursue your loss, *ie* the profit you would have made. You cannot claim for meals you did not provide and which were not spoilt.

A letter sent by recorded delivery, formally requiring payment, should be written first and a copy kept for your records. This letter should end, 'Unless payment in full is received by. . . (giving seven to ten days) a summons will be taken out against you in the County Court. In this event, the above amount will be enhanced by the Court fee.' Be very firm — you don't want this sort of guest to make another booking.

Such a letter will usually be enough to get payment on its way to you. If not, booklets detailing the procedure for small claims (less than £3,000) and for enforcing judgements are available from County Courts in England, Wales and Northern Ireland, from Sheriff Courts in Scotland and from Citizens Advice Bureaux.

Small claims procedures are generally informal and you need not employ a solicitor. If the client is in the wrong and your letter did not work, the issue of a summons will in the vast majority of cases have the desired effect since the defendant has only about 14 days to either pay the money into court or enter a defence. Bear in mind, however, it is no advantage to obtain judgement if the debtor has no money.

You will now see good reason for requiring deposits whenever possible and for getting accounts settled other than by unguaranteed cheques.

FINAL HINTS

- Know what you're doing.
- Work hard at being a success.
- If financial problems should loom, get help *immediately* (Business Links have a 'troubleshooter service').

And remember:

- the right attitude, plus
- good food, plus
- high standards of comfort and cleanliness, equals
- contented guests, equals
- repeat bookings and recommendations, equals
- full bedspaces, equals
- **profit**.

CHECKLIST

Have you:

- Set the tone for your hotel?
- Decided on the house rules?
- Decided the level of service to offer?
- Decided what facilities to offer?
- Decided on your menus?
- Ensured your hotel is different?

Do you:

- Know how to assess the competition?
- Know how to run a bar?
- Know the law relating to hotels?
- Know how to take a booking?
- Know how to deal with the ensuing correspondence?
- Know how to keep ahead of the competition?
- Know how to pursue losses?
- Know how to stay profitable?
- Have the determination to succeed?

Food for thought

You will not please all of the people all of the time. If you please most of the people most of the time, you will be a success.

HOW DO YOU SURVIVE IN A RECESSION?

Recessions in business, whether major ones like a downturn in the economy or minor ones like spells of bad weather, can and will affect your livelihood from time to time. Those who have over-borrowed are worst affected.

Much of the advice given so far is designed to make you run your business professionally and cost-effectively. This is always important but particularly so when visitors are thin on the ground.

Many hoteliers, noticeably those at the lower end of the scale, show a marked failure to appreciate the needs of the market, in particular the standards required. In other words, they are nowhere near professional enough.

Even in bad times, a number of businesses continue to thrive. Ask yourself why. They are the ones doing things right. A need always exists for good hotel accommodation and if you have chosen your location carefully and stand out from the crowd, yours will be one of those businesses which thrives in almost any circumstances. It requires much effort and a determination to succeed, plus:

- the right attitude: impress your guests at all times
- knowledge of your job, your market, the law
- control over your cash flow, your business strategy.

Respond to your competitors if necessary by offering for example bargain breaks and other inducements. Diversify (see page 144) if you can.

In keeping your finances under control:

- carefully assess stock levels and keep nothing that does not sell well
- lay off or cut back hours of staff without allowing sentiment to intervene if it's your survival at stake
- ruthlessly cut out advertisements that don't pay their way.

Even in the poorest of seasons, never:

- reduce your tariff below viable level
- cut corners (your guests will be the first to notice)
- panic (remember the £5,000 advertisement?).

If in spite of everything survival is in doubt, get immediate advice from:

- Business Link
- your accountant
- your local hotel or trade association.

If survival in a recession is an achievement, just think what you can achieve in better times!

Appendix of
Further Information

RELEVANT ACTS OF PARLIAMENT

The following are some of the most important Acts of Parliament and Orders/Regulations made under them, parts of which have an effect on the running of hotels.

Business Names Act 1985
Requires the disclosure of business ownership where the owner's name is not the same as the business name. A notice must be displayed and the information shown on various documents. (Page 86).

Consumer Protection Act 1987
Consumers may not be misled as to prices, nor must a price rise after it has been quoted (excluding rises in VAT). (Page 100).

Control of Substances Hazardous to Health Regulations 1994
Part of the health and safety at work legislation. Requires owners to take notice of substances which may cause injury or illness to employees. (Page 106.)

Copyright, Designs and Patents Act 1988
Restricts public performances of material, the copyright of which is owned by, *eg*, composers and record companies, and entitles designated companies to claim fees in the form of licences. (Page 93.)

Credit Cards (Price Discrimination) Order 1990
Makes it an offence for *credit card* companies to prohibit merchants from discriminating regarding payments made by credit card. (Page 136.)

Data Protection Act 1998
Requires that data held on computer must be made available to the public

and that owners must notify the Data Protection Commissioner. Manual records and their accessibility plus CCTV data are also covered. (Page 83).

Development of Tourism Act 1969
Enables the Tourist Board in Wales to offer grants for projects connected with tourism. (Page 61.)

Disability Discrimination Act 1995
Provides rights for disabled guests. (Page 30.)

Electrical Equipment (Safety) Regulations 1994
Lay down standards for safety, maintenance and use of equipment and appliances. (Page 92.)

Employer's Liability (Compulsory Insurance) Act 1969
Requires employers to insure their employees and to display an up-to-date certificate of insurance. (Page 77.)

Equal Pay Act 1970
Prohibits discrimination between sexes in relation to rates of pay. (Page 108.)

Fire Prevention Act 1971
Fire Precautions (Workplace) Regulations 1997 and 1999
Lay down requirements as regards the necessity for a fire certificate, the provision of equipment, and for the fire risks to be assessed and acted upon. (Pages 41 and 43.)

Food Labelling Regulations 1996
Require food to be labelled accurately. (Page 43.)

Food Safety Act 1990
Food Safety (General Food Hygiene) Regulations 1995
Food Safety (Temperature Control) Regulations 1995
Lay down standards for all aspects of food safety, kitchen and equipment hygiene. (Pages 43–4.)

Furniture and Furnishings (Fire) (Safety) Regulations 1988 (as amended)
Make requirements for fire retardant standards in furniture, etc. (Page 43.)

Gas Safety (Installation and Use) Regulations 1994
Lay down standards for safety, maintenance and use of equipment and appliances. (Page 92.)

Health & Safety (Safety Signs and Signals) Regulations 1996
Specify format of signs in respect of fire to be displayed, in particular fire exit signs. (Page 43.)

Health and Safety at Work, *etc* Act 1974
Lays down standards for the health and safety of the public and employees. Many health and safety type sets of Regulations are made under this Act. (Page 106.)

Health and Safety Information for Employees Regulations 1989
Require employees to be notified of health and safety requirements either by poster or by individual leaflets. (Page 107.)

Hotel Proprietors Act 1956
Hotel Proprietors (Northern Ireland) Act 1958
Require proprietor's liability regarding guests' property to be set out in a prominently displayed notice. (Pages 79–80.)

Immigration (Hotel Records) Order 1972
Requires guests to register and records to be kept for inspection. (Page 147.)

Law of Property Act 1925
Sets out the continuing obligations of lessees during the life of the lease. (Page 48.)

Licensing Acts 1964 and 1988
Licensing (Scotland) Act 1976
Set out legislation regarding the supply and consumption of intoxicating liquor. (Pages 156-7.)

Management of Health and Safety at Work Regulations 1999
Oblige you to assess hazards and risks. (Page 107.)

National Minimum Wage Act 1998
Sets out who should receive what and gives formulae for working out the effect of providing staff accommodation, and also guidance on tips. Page 108.)

Price Indications (Method of Payment) Regulations 1991
Require notices at entrances and at payment points where different prices are charged for payment by credit card. (Page 136.)

Price Marking (Food and Drink on Premises) Order 1979.
Requires prior notice to be given to the public in the form of a tariff before entering serving area. (Does not apply to residents.) (Page 101.)

Provisions and Use of Work Equipment Regulations 1998
Cover suitability, use etc of equipment. (Page 92.)

Race Relations Act 1976
Makes it an offence to discriminate on grounds of race. (Pages 103 and 104.)

Reporting of Injuries, Diseases and Occurrences Regulations 1995
Made under health and safety legislation. Require notification of injuries, etc. (Page 107.)

Sex Discrimination Act 1975
Part of employment legislation. Prohibits selection of staff on basis of gender, also protects married women. (Page 104.)

Tourism (Sleeping Accommodation Price Display) Order 1977
Requires tariff to be displayed if there are four or more bedrooms or at least eight beds. (Page 100.)

Trade Descriptions Act 1968
Requires all descriptions to be accurate. (Page 100.)

Transfer of Undertakings (Protection of Employment) Regulations 1981, as amended
Detail the rights of staff when a business changes hands. (Page 102.)

Weights and Measures Act 1985
Weights and Measures (Intoxicating Liquor) Order 1988
Lay down the quantities and conditions under which intoxicating liquor may be served. (Pages 96 and 150.)

Working Time Regulations 1998

Set out working time limits (the 48-hour week) plus rest periods, leave entitlements, etc. (Page 106.)

Workplace (Health, Safety and Welfare) Regulations 1992

Detail your obligations to assess hazards and risks. (Page 107.)

TRADE MAGAZINES

As a hotelier, it is a distinct advantage to take one of the numerous trade magazines. They keep you up to date with the frequent changes in legislation, catering exhibitions, the latest developments in equipment, etc and many other matters which affect the industry.

Caterer and Hotelkeeper, weekly. Available from newsagents and by subscription from Reed Business Information Ltd. Tel: (01444) 445566. Fax: (01444) 445447.

Catering Update, monthly. Free to caterers with purchasing power. Reed Business Information Ltd. Tel: (020) 8652 8307.

Hospitality, ten pa. The official magazine of the Hotel & Catering International Management Association. Distributed free to members, also available on subscription. For address, etc, see under **Trade Associations**, below.

Hospitality Matters, seven pa. The 'house' magazine of the British Hospitality Association. Distributed free to members, also available on subscription. For address, etc, see under **Trade Associations**, below.

Hotel & Restaurant Magazine, monthly. Controlled circulation. Free to hotel managers, directors and decision makers. Quantum Publishing, Quantum House, 19 Scarbrook Road, Croydon CR9 1LX. Tel: (020) 8565 4200. Fax: (020) 8565 4202.

Independent Caterer, monthly. Controlled circulation to those in the catering industry. Datateam Publishing Ltd, London Road, Maidstone, Kent ME16 8LY. Tel: (01622) 687031. Fax: (01622) 757646. Email: caterer@datateam.co.uk

Some other magazines specialise in public houses and restaurants. Others are issued on a national or regional basis.

USEFUL ADDRESSES

The inclusion of any organisation which is run commercially is not intended as a recommendation, nor does exclusion imply anything adverse.

Trade Associations

British Hospitality Association, Queens House, 55/56 Lincoln's Inn Fields, London WC2A 3BH. Tel: (020) 7404 7744. Fax: (020) 7404 7799. Web: www.bha-online.org.uk

British Institute of Innkeeping, 80 Park Street, Camberley, Surrey GU15 3PT. Tel: (01276) 684449. Fax: (01276) 23045. Web: www. barzone.co.uk

Federation of Small Businesses, Whittle Way, Blackpool Business Park, Blackpool FY4 2FE. Tel: (01253) 336000. Fax: (01253) 348046. Web: www.fsb.org.uk

Forum of Private Business, Ruskin Chambers, Drury Lane, Knutsford, Cheshire WA16 6HA. Tel: (01565) 634467. Fax: (01565) 650059. Web: www.fpb.co.uk

Hotel & Catering International Management Association, 191 Trinity Road, London SW17 7HN. Tel: (020) 8672 4251. Fax: (020) 8682 1710. Web: http://hcima.org.uk/

National Council of Hotel Associations, PO Box 2309, Bath BA2 6XN. Tel: (01225) 835088. Fax: (01225) 837900. Web: www.bed-and-breakfast.org

About professional advisors

Association of Chartered Certified Accountants, 29 Lincoln's Inn Fields, London WC2A 3EE. Tel: (020) 7242 6855. Fax: (020) 7831 8054. Web: www.acca.org.uk

Institute of Chartered Accountants, PO Box 433, Moorgate Place, London EC2P 2BJ. Tel: (020) 7920 8100. Fax: (020) 7920 0547. Web: www.icaew.co.uk

Institute of Chartered Accountants of Scotland, 27 Queen Street, Edinburgh EH2 1LA. Tel: (0131) 225 5673. Fax: (0131) 225 3813. Web: www.icas.org.uk

The Law Society, 113 Chancery Lane, London WC2A 1PL. Tel: (020) 7242 1222. Fax: (020) 7320 5964. Web: www.lawsociety.org.uk

Royal Institution of Chartered Surveyors (now incorporating the Incorporated Society of Valuers and Auctioneers), 12 Gt George Street, Parliament Square, London SW1P 3AD. Tel: (020) 7222 7000. Fax: (020) 7222 9430. Web: www.rics.org.uk

Advice on assistance and grants

Department of Trade and Industry, 1–19 Victoria Street, London SW1H
0ET. Tel: (020) 7215 5000. Fax: (020) 7222 0612.

DTI Small/Medium Enterprise Policy Unit (deals with the Loan
Guarantee Scheme), St Mary's House, Level 2, c/o Moorfoot,
Sheffield S1 4PQ. Tel: (08700) 010172.

English Partnerships (leasing of property for business projects), St
George's House, Kingsway, Team Valley, Gateshead, Tyne and Wear
NE11 0NA. Tel: (0191) 487 8941. Fax: (0191) 487 5690.

Highlands and Islands Enterprise, Bridge House, 20 Bridge Street,
Inverness IV1 1QR. Tel: (01463) 234171. Fax: (01463) 244469.

Local Enterprise Agencies. Obtain address from: Department of the
Environment, Tel: (020) 7890 3755; Scottish Business Shop
Network, Tel: (0800) 787878; Business Connect Wales, Tel: (0345)
969798; LEDU (Northern Ireland), Tel: (01232) 491031.

Welsh Development Agency, Principality House, The Friary, Cardiff
CF1 4AE. Tel: (0345) 775577. Fax: (01443) 845589.

Advice on training/student grants

Business Link. For your local office in England, telephone the
Signposting Line on (08457) 567765. For Northern Ireland, Scotland
and Wales see under Local Enterprise Agencies, above.

Employment Service. See telephone directory for regional offices and
local Jobcentres.

Hospitality Training Foundation 3rd Floor, International House, High
Street, Ealing, London W5 5DB. Helpline: (090668) 443322..

Hotel and Catering Training Company, 10th Floor, 26–28 Hammersmith
Grove, London W6 7HT. Tel: (020) 7735 9700. Fax: (020) 7735
9701. Web: www.hctc.co.uk

Scottish Qualification Authority, Hanover House, 24 Douglas Street,
Glasgow G2 7NQ. Tel: (0141) 242 2198. Fax: (0141) 242 2244.

Local Universities and Colleges of Further Education.

Advice on employment and staff

Advisory, Conciliation & Arbitration Service (ACAS). See telephone
directory for regional offices and Public Enquiry Points.

Employment Service. See under Advice on training/student grants.

Equal Opportunities Commission, Overseas House, Quay Street,
Manchester M3 3HN. Tel: (0161) 833 9244. Fax: (0161) 835 1657.
Email: info@eoc.org.uk

Health & Safety Executive Library and Information Services, Broad
Lane, Sheffield S3 7HQ; St Hugh's House, Stanley Precinct, Trinity

Road, Bootle L20 3QY. Access through HSE InfoLine (0541) 545500. Rose Court, 2 Southwark Bridge, London SE1 9HS. Tel: (020) 7717 6000. Fax: (020) 7717 6717.

Racial Equality, the Commission for, Elliott House, 10–12 Allington Street, London SW1E 5EH. Tel: (020) 7828 7022. Fax: (020) 7630 7605. Email: info@cre.gov.uk

Tourist Boards

English (Tourism Council): Thames Tower, Black's Road, London W6 9EL. Tel: (020) 8563 3000. Fax: (020) 8563 0302. Web: www. englishtourism.org.uk

Northern Ireland: St Anne's Court, 59 North Street, Belfast BT1 1NB. Tel: (01232) 231221. Fax: (01232) 240960. Email: info@nitb.com

Scottish: 23 Ravelstone Terrace, Edinburgh EH4 3EU. Tel: (0131) 332 2433. Fax: (0131) 431513. Email: info@stb.gov.uk

Wales: Brunel House, 2 Fitzalan Road, Cardiff CF2 1UY. Tel: (029) 2049 9909. Fax: (029) 2048 5031.

Cumbria: Ashleigh, Holly Road, Windermere LA23 2AQ. Tel: (015394) 44444. Fax: (015394) 440441. Email: mail@cumbria-tourist-board.co.uk

East of England: Topplesfield Hall, Hadleigh, Suffolk IP7 5DN. Tel: (01473) 822922. Fax: (01473) 823063. Email: eastofenglandtouristboard@compuserve.com

Heart of England: Larkhill Road, Worcester WR5 2EZ. Tel: (01905) 763436. Fax: (01905) 763450. Web: www.visitbritain.com/heart-of-england

London (and Convention Bureau): 6th Floor, Glen House, Stag Place, London SW1E 5LT. Tel: (020) 7932 2000. Fax: (020) 7932 2222. Email: enquiries@londontouristboard.co.uk

Northumbria: Aykley Heads, Durham City, Durham DH1 5UX. Tel: (0191) 375 3000. Fax: (0191) 386 0899. Email: enquiries@ntb.org.uk

North West: Swan House, Swan Meadow Road, Wigan Pier, Wigan WN3 5BB. Tel: (01942) 821222. Fax: (01942) 820002. Email: info@nwtb.org.uk

South East England: The Old Brew House, Warwick Park, Tunbridge Wells, Kent TN2 5TU. Tel: (01892) 540766. Fax: (01892) 511008. Email: enquiries@setb.org.uk

South West Tourism: 60 St David's Hill, Exeter, Devon EX4 4SY. Tel: (01392) 425426. Fax: (0870) 442 0840. Email: post@swtourism.co.uk

Southern: 40 Chamberlayne Road, Eastleigh, Hampshire SO50 5JH.
Tel: (023) 8065 2000. Fax: (023) 8061 0286.
Email: 100651.3040@compuserve.com
Yorkshire: 312 Tadcaster Road, York YO2 2HF. Tel: (01904) 707961.
Fax: (01904) 701414. Email: ytb@ytb.org.uk

Miscellaneous

Advertising Standards Authority, Brook House, 2–16 Torrington Place,
London WC1E 7HN. Tel: (020) 7580 5555. Fax: (020) 7631 3051.
Web: www.asa.org.uk

Companies Registration Office (England and Wales), Companies House,
Crown Way, Maindy, Cardiff CF4 3UZ. Tel: (029) 2038 0801. Fax:
(029) 2038 0517. Email: emailenquiries@companieshouse.gov.uk

Companies Registration Office (Scotland), Companies House, 37 Castle
Terrace, Edinburgh EH1 2EB. Tel: (0131) 535 5800. Fax: (0131) 535
5820. Web: www.companieshouse.gov.uk

Data Protection Commissioner, Wycliffe House, Water Lane, Wilmslow,
Cheshire SK9 5AF. Tel: (01625) 545745. Fax: (01625) 524510.
Email: data@wycliffe.demon.co.uk

Farm Holiday Guide Publications Ltd, Abbey Mill Business Centre,
Paisley PA1 1TJ. Tel: (0141) 887 0428. Fax: (0141) 889 7204. Email:
fhg@ipc.co.uk

Office of Fair Trading, Fleetbank House, 2–6 Salisbury Square, London
EC4Y 8JX. Tel: (020) 7211 8000. Fax: (020) 7211 8800. Web:
www.oft.gov.uk

Performing Right Society, Elwes House, 19 Church Walk, Peterborough
PE1 2UZ. Tel: (0800) 0684828. Fax: (01733) 312912. Web:
www.prs.co.uk

Phonographic Performance Ltd, 1 Upper James Street, London W1R
3HG. Tel: (020) 7534 1000. Fax: (020) 7534 1111. Web:
www.ppluk.com

Registry of Companies, Credit Unions and Industrial & Provident
Societies. (Northern Ireland) 64 Chichester Street, Belfast, BT1 4JX.
Tel: (01232) 544820. Fax: (01232) 544888.

FURTHER READING

Computer Systems in the Hotel & Catering Industry, B Brabham.
Creating a Web Site, Bruce Durie (How To Books).
Do Your Own Advertising, Michael Bennie (How To Books).
Employ and Manage Staff, Wendy Wyatt (How To Books).
Hotel & Catering Law in Britain, David Field (Sweet & Maxwell).

How to Buy Your Own Hotel, Miles Quest (Hutchinson).
Kitchen Planning & Management, John Fuller and David Kirk (Butterworth Heinemann).
Managing Through People, John Humphries (How To Books).
Managing Your Business Accounts, Peter Taylor (How To Books).
Running Your Own Small Hotel, J Lennick.
Setting Up Your Own Limited Company, Robert Browning (How To Books).
Starting Your Own Business, Jim Green (How To Books).
Starting Up Your Own Business in the Hotel & Catering Industry, Hotel & Catering Training Board.
Taking On Staff, David Greenwood (How To Books).
Working in Hotels & Catering, Mark Hempshell (How To Books).

ETC CLASSIFICATIONS

Quality standards for guest accommodation and the national accessible scheme for serviced & self-catering accommodation

The following pages contain the rating requirements for a Quality Standard for 'Guest Accommodation'. It encompasses Guest Houses, Farmhouses, Inns, Bed and Breakfasts and other establishments which may not be eligible for the Hotel Standard. The standards are based on research into the needs and expectations of visitors.

Also included is the National Accessible Scheme, which is operated by the national tourist board for England, Scotland and Wales. This identifies and acknowledges those places to stay that meet the needs of wheelchair users and others with limited mobility.

For those of you requiring a star rating (similar to the old AA/RAC stars), requirements are listed in a Quality Standards for Hotels brochure which may be obtained free of charge from the ETC, Regional Tourist Boards, the AA or the RAC.

QUALITY STANDARDS FOR GUEST ACCOMMODATION

Introduction

This booklet contains the rating requirements for a Quality Standard for 'Guest Accommodation'. It encompasses Guesthouses, Farmhouses, Inns, Bed and Breakfasts and other establishments which may not be eligible for the Hotel Standard. The standards are based on research into the needs and expectations of visitors.

Minimum Requirements for Guest Accommodation

To be recognised within this 'Guest Accommodation' standard an establishment must meet **all** the **'Minimum Entry Requirements'** listed throughout this booklet.

Additionally an establishment must provide sufficient quality to merit a minimum score of **'1'** in all areas of operation covered by the **'Quality Indicators'** listed throughout this booklet.

Assessment for Quality Rating

Establishments recognised will be given a quality rating on a scale of 1 to 5. Assessments to arrive at this rating will be based primarily on guest care and the quality of what is offered, rather than the provision of extra facilities.

Assessing the Quality Score

All aspects of an establishment will be given a **'Quality Score'** during the inspection process. Some areas of assessment are given additional weighting to reflect their importance to the consumer.

An overall score for quality is established which is then converted to a percentage. This percentage score is then used to determine the quality rating to be awarded against pre set bandings.

Quality Indicators

Examples are given of the level of quality expected to achieve a quality score from

1 to 5 for each area of assessment. Where phrases such as adequate, good, very good etc are used, these signify ascending levels of quality in broad terms only. They are deliberately non-specific, recognising the wide variety of quality elements that could be included.

The **'Quality Indicators'** represent typical expectations. They are neither definitive or exhaustive.

The rating awarded actually will allow for a balanced view of the hospitality, accommodation, food and services, provided by an establishment. It may be limited where, in an important area, such as cleanliness or guest care, the minimum entry level is not exceeded. Diamonds are awarded as follows:

Rating Levels

Level 1 Quality % of 20%-34% ◆
Level 2 Quality % of 35%-49% ◆◆
Level 3 Quality % of 50%-69% ◆◆◆
Level 4 Quality % of 70%-84% ◆◆◆◆
Level 5 Quality % of 85%+ ◆◆◆◆◆

How a Quality Rating is assessed within the Guest Accommodation Standard 'The Mystery Inn'

Area Assessed	Maximum Score	Score Achieved
Cleanliness	75	60
Guest Care	60	30
Bedrooms	40	26
Bathrooms	30	17
Food Quality	30	15
Public Areas	20	14
General Requirements	25	16
Total	**280**	**178**

In this example the 'Mystery Inn' scored 178 out of a possible 280, which gives a quality percentage of 64%. **A Quality Rating Level 3 would be awarded.**

Quality Standard Scores

The following sliding scale indicates the type of factors required to achieve various levels of Quality Score.

Quality Score	1	2	3	4	5
Quality Indicators	Factors which indicate the minimum level of acceptability quality		Factors which indicate a Quality Score of 3.		Factors which indicate a Quality Score of 5.

1 Cleanliness

Cleanliness

Minimum Entry Requirements	Cleanliness is of paramount importance to guests in all types of establishment, so a high standard of cleanliness must be achieved and maintained throughout the property. Particular attention given to bathrooms, shower rooms and toilets and items involving direct contact for guests, such as bedding, linen, towels, baths, showers, washbasins, WCs, flooring, seating, crockery, cutlery and glassware.

All bedrooms and bathrooms cleaned daily.

Quality Score	1	2	3	4	5
Quality Indicators	All surfaces clean and free from dust. All rooms vacuumed daily. Guest areas kept tidy.		Evidence of attention to detail, particularly high and low level dusting. Clean and freshly polished surfaces. All areas free from clutter. Soft furnishings and carpets cleaned on a regular basis. All areas smelling fresh and clean.		Clearly a pristine finish. Gleaming surfaces, no smears or marks; evidence of thorough cleaning. Spotless soft furnishings and carpets.

2 Service and hospitality – Guest care

Bookings and prices

Minimum Entry Requirements	To make clear to guests exactly what is included in the prices quoted for accommodation, meals and refreshments, including service charge, taxes and other surcharges.

To describe fairly to all guests and prospective guests the amenities, facilities and services provided by the establishment, whether by advertisement, brochure, word of mouth or any other means. Details of any in-house policies, eg no smoking, should be communicated at time of booking. Allow guests to see the accommodation, if requested, before booking.

Details of charges for additional services or facilities available should be explained, including cancellation terms, if any.

Quality Score	1	2	3	4	5
Quality Indicators	Competent telephone manner when taking bookings. Basic details recorded (guest names, address, tel. no., dates of stay, number of single/double rooms required etc).		A positive and friendly attitude from proprietors and staff handling bookings. Organised approach for dealing with guest enquiries, reservations, correspondence, complaints etc.		Efficient booking, with helpful and friendly telephone manner. Confirmation letter and directions sent by post/fax.

2 Service and hospitality – Guest care

Guest arrival and access

Minimum Entry Requirements

Proprietor or staff to be on duty during guests' arrival and departure periods and during meal times.

To provide service appropriate to the style of accommodation, and to deal promptly with all enquiries, requests, reservations, correspondence and complaints from guests.

An effective means for guests to call for the attention of proprietor or staff who should be available at all reasonable times.

Once guests have registered, they should have access to the establishment and to their bedrooms at all times unless restrictions were previously notified. It is acceptable that the entrance may be locked and the guests may have to ring or knock for access or be given a key. Guests should be made aware of any restrictions at the time of booking.

Quality Score	I	2	3	4	5
Quality Indicators	Guests made to feel welcome on arrival with no undue delays checking in. Polite proprietors and staff, willing to help when asked. Tidy appearance of proprietors and staff.		Good registration procedures. Sincere, courteous and well presented proprietors and staff. All requests dealt with pleasantly.		Prompt, thorough registration with a professional approach. Smartly presented proprietors and staff. All necessary information offered to guests. Warm, cheerful welcome on arrival, with offer of refreshment. An excellent first impression, establishing a good rapport with guests. Appropriate use of guests' names.
	Guests directed to their rooms.		Guests shown to their rooms. Assistance with luggage offered.		Guests escorted to their rooms and given assistance with luggage. Guests made to feel at home and encouraged to make any additional requests known. Well trained, knowledgeable and enthusiastic proprietors and staff showing very good levels of attention and anticipating guest needs. Genuinely helpful attitude; nothing too much trouble.

7

2 Service and hospitality – Guest care

Breakfast/Dining room service (where appropriate) See also Public Areas – General and Breakfast/Dining room

Quality Score	1	2	3	4	5
Quality Indicators	Competent service with helpful attitude.	Attentive, friendly service with good levels of customer care.		Prompt and efficient service with excellent levels of customer care and good technical skills.	
	Reasonable product knowledge.	Good product knowledge.		Comprehensive descriptions of dishes available.	
	Tables laid appropriately for the meal being served.			Proprietors and staff able to provide advice on menu and wine list (where provided) for guests.	

Guest departure

Minimum Entry Requirements

To provide each visitor, on request, with details of payments due and a receipt, if required.

Presentation and layout of the bill should be clearly detailed.

Quality Score	1	2	3	4	5
Quality Indicators	No undue delays for guests on departure.	Efficient procedures for handling guest departure.		Prompt attention, with friendly and cheerful handling of guest departure. Offer of assistance with luggage.	
	Proprietors and staff willing to assist if bill is unclear or inaccurate.	Accurate bill, proprietors and staff well versed in all methods of payment (where appropriate).		Bill correct in all details and professionally presented.	
		Good last impression.		Excellent last impression.	

3 Bedrooms – Guest comfort

Bedroom size – space and comfort

Minimum Entry Requirements

All bedrooms and bathrooms having sufficient space to allow freedom of movement to guests.

In assessing the acceptability of bedroom size, inspectors will take account of usable space available around furnishings and fittings. It is unlikely that the minimum requirements will be met where bedroom sizes are less than the following:

Single	5.6 sq m/60 sq ft
Double	8.4 sq m/90 sq ft
Twin	10.2 sq m/110 sq ft

Additionally, for a quality score higher than the base level score of 1, room sizes will need to be greater with significantly more usable space around furnishings and fittings.

Rooms for family occupation will be significantly larger.

Fully openable doors and drawers. The ceiling height for the major part of the room sufficient for a person of 6ft to move around without stooping. Sloping eaves and roofs are acceptable providing these do not restrict guests' movement to an unacceptable degree.

Quality Score	1	2	3	4	5
Quality Indicators	Reasonable free movement not to be unduly restricted by intrusive low beams.		Sufficient space to allow free movement and a good degree of comfort.		Ample space to allow free movement and a high degree of comfort. Area available for luggage storage without cluttering the room and obstructing access.
	Uncluttered rooms.		Easy use of facilities.		
			Convenient lay-out of furniture for practical use.		Easy and convenient use of facilities, eg use of surfaces without moving tea tray or TV (where provided), access to power points etc.
			TV (where provided) visible from sitting area or bed.		TV (where provided) visible from sitting area and bed.
	Suitable seating in sound condition for the type and style of accommodation.		Practical, comfortable chairs.		Comfortable easy chairs.
			Access to both sides of a double bed.		Generous access to both sides of a double bed.
	Reasonable sound insulation with minimal intrusive noise from plumbing, corridors etc.				No intrusive noise.

9

3 Bedrooms – Guest comfort

Beds and bedding – size and quality

Minimum Entry Requirements

Minimum bed sizes: (except childrens' beds in family rooms)
Single   190 x 90 cm/6'3" x 3'
Double   190 x 137cm/6'3"x 4'6"

NB Where existing establishments currently provide 2'6"x6' single and/or 4'x6' double beds for adults, they will be allowed until 1 July 2000 to upgrade to the dimensions specified above.

All mattresses to be of sprung interior, foam or similar quality, modern and comfortable, with mattress protectors and/or underblankets.

All beds to be of sound condition with a secure headboard or equivalent.

All beds made daily.

All bed linen, including duvet covers, changed at least weekly and for each new guest.

All bedding to be clean and in sufficient quantity, according to season and guests' needs. As a guide, two good quality blankets per bed and two pillows in individual pillowcases per person are required as well as a quilt or third blanket and bedspread.

Spare pillows and blankets available on request.

Duvets are acceptable. Additional bedding should be available on request.

100% man-made fibre sheets are unacceptable.

Quality Score	1	2	3
Quality Indicators	Acceptable quality bed and mattress. Plastic or rubber mattress protectors tolerated but not encouraged on adult beds.	Good quality comfortable bed, firm mattresses and sound base. Bed frames may be of older style, but in good condition.	Excellent quality bed, eg sprung mattress and high quality base; clean headboard offering a high degree of comfort.
	Adequately presented beds with clean linen and bed covers in good repair. Adequate range of bedding, including sufficient blankets. Additional bedding provided in guest rooms should be clean and fresh, preferably wrapped.	Well presented beds, with good quality, freshly laundered, co-ordinated linen and bedding. Bed linen changed at least every 4 days except where, as part of an environmental policy, guests are invited to agree to less frequent changes of linen. Ample good quality bedding, including extra pillows and blankets.	Co-ordinated and crisply laundered linen changed at least every 2 days. A choice of bedding available eg thickly quilted, or similar quality bedspreads and blankets, or duvets with appropriate tog rating, All of a high quality and co-ordinated with bedroom decor and other soft furnishings. Allergy-free pillows to be available. High standard of overall presentation – appropriate use of valences, pillows and cushions. May offer evening turn-down service.

3 Bedrooms – Guest comfort

Decoration

Quality Score	1	2	3	4	5
Quality Indicators	Functional decor and limited co-ordination.		Co-ordinated interior design.		Excellent interior design, with high attention to detail. Thoughtful co-ordination of patterns, colours and textures.
			Well finished, good quality wall coverings and paintwork. Wall and ceiling coverings well applied.		High quality wall coverings with professional finish to all aspects of decoration.
			Use of pictures etc where appropriate, particularly on plain walls.		Attractive use of pictures, prints and other decorative relief.

Furniture, furnishings and fittings

Minimum Entry Requirements

Bedside or bedhead table, cabinet or shelf to be provided for all beds.

A dressing table or equivalent, with a mirror adjacent, to be provided.

A chair or stool.

If a lounge is not available, a comfortable chair should be provided for reading etc.

A wardrobe or clothes hanging space with sufficient hangers per person. An alcove is acceptable but hooks on walls or behind doors are not.

Wire hangers are not acceptable.

Adequate drawer or shelf space available.

Drawers should run freely and should be lined or have an easily wiped surface.

Quality Score	1	2	3	4	5
Quality Indicators	A sparing but adequate provision of furniture, furnishings and fittings in terms of quality and range; limited co-ordination.		Good quality furniture, in a sound and useable condition.		Excellent quality modern, reproduction or antique furniture. Furniture of sound construction.
			Good use of co-ordination. Size and amount of furnishings in proportion to the space available.		Excellent co-ordination of furniture and plush, soft furnishings of high intrinsic quality.
					Additional features such as scatter cushions.

3 Bedrooms – Guest comfort

Windows and window dressings

Minimum Entry Requirements	At least one window with clear glass to provide natural light and adequate ventilation. If windows are sealed, air conditioning must be provided.
	Acceptable quality opaque curtains, blinds or shutters should be provided on all windows, including glass panels to doors, fanlights and sky-light windows to afford both privacy and exclusion of light. Applies also to bathrooms, shower rooms and toilets.
	Where bedrooms are located on the ground floor, consideration should be given to providing additional privacy in the form of a net curtain or blind.

Quality Score	1	2	3	4	5
Quality Indicators	All window coverings correctly fitted.		Substantial lined curtains with sufficient width and height to draw completely across the window.	Window dressing denoting a degree of luxury with good use of pelmets and tie-backs, ample drape and width. Curtains to be fully lined so as to retain heat and keep out light.	

Heating

Minimum Entry Requirements	Adequate in-room heating provided at no extra cost.
	Extra heating to be available on request at no extra charge.

Quality Score	1	2	3	4	5
Quality Indicators	Heating levels appropriate to the size of bedroom.		Effective levels of heating providing overall uniform temperature. Properly fitted, thermostatically controlled heating.	Properly fitted individual thermostatic controlled heating. Equipment in excellent condition. Bedrooms heated and/or ventilated prior to guests' arrival. In hot weather, fans available, on request, for guest comfort.	

3 Bedrooms – Guest comfort

Lighting

Minimum Entry Requirements

Bedrooms and bathrooms should be well lit.

As guidance, overall lighting levels of 160 watts for a single room and 220 watts for a double room.

A bedroom light to be controlled from the door, and additionally a means of controlling a light from each bed.

All bulbs, unless decorative, should have a shade or cover.

Quality Score	1	2	3	4	5
Quality Indicators	Light fittings of adequate quality for the style, size, and shape of the bedroom. Adequate natural light.		Well positioned lights giving good levels of illumination. Good quality light fittings with appropriate shades. Ample natural light.		Variety of quality lights, well positioned and suitable for all purposes. Controllable lighting, giving variable levels of light as appropriate.

Flooring

Minimum Entry Requirements

Acceptable quality fully fitted carpets, or where an acceptable alternative flooring is provided, slip resistant rugs or mats placed by the bedside.

Quality Score	1	2	3	4	5
Quality Indicators	Adequate comfort to flooring.		Well fitted, good quality flooring in sound condition and comfortable under foot.		Professionally fitted, high quality carpeting (eg high percentage wool content, in excellent condition) or polished floorboards with rugs.

3 Bedrooms – Guest comfort

Other bedroom facilities and services

Minimum Entry Requirements

Beverage making

If beverage making facilities are not provided in the bedroom or available on request, service of hot beverages should be available morning and evening.

Where in-room facilities are provided, attention should be given to ensure that a kettle can be used safely.

Fresh milk should be available on request and consumables kept wrapped or in lidded containers.

Telephone

Where a payphone is not available, the guests should, on request, be able to make or receive phone calls on the proprietor's own telephone. The proprietor may of course charge for this facility.

Where facilities are provided, all charges must be clearly indicated. Where costs are shown per unit, the duration of the unit must be explained to ensure that the guest has a fair indication of the probable total cost of the call.

Miscellaneous

A waste paper container (non-flammable if smoking is permitted).

An ashtray (where smoking is permitted).

A drinking tumbler per guest. This should be clear glass, scratchless plastic or wrapped disposable.

A towel rail or equivalent with hand and bath towels (one of each) provided per person. Fresh soap provided for each new letting. Where liquid soap dispensers are used, particular attention needs to be paid to their cleanliness and hygiene.

Sufficient conveniently situated power sockets to allow for the safe use of all electrical equipment provided.

Printed advice on how to obtain emergency assistance at night by means of a notice or indication within the room information. This requirement is in addition to the fire instruction notice.

Iron and ironing board available on request.

Early morning calls available on request or alarm clocks in bedrooms.

Extra bedroom facilities and accessories

These are facilities and accessories which may be provided within the bedroom, they are not requirements, but if provided the quality, range, presentation and ease of use will all be taken into account in the assessment.

Quality Score	1	2	3	4
Quality Indicators	Very limited range of additional facilities and accessories, if any.		Good range of additional facilities and accessories.	Excellent range of additional facilities and accessories.

Examples of facilities

In-room beverage-making equipment, colour television and radio, hairdrier, additional guest information, full-length mirror, luggage rack (where provided without charge) and items such as telephones (on a pay-for-use basis).

Examples of accessories

Complimentary bottled water, fresh flowers or plants, reading material, biscuits and sweets, where provided freely.

4 Bathrooms, shower rooms and en-suite facilities etc.

General

Minimum Entry Requirements – Overall

All bathrooms cleaned daily. Particular attention should be given to items involving direct contact for guests, such as towels, baths, showers, washbasins, WCs, flooring, seating and glassware.

At least one bath or shower room with washbasin for every **six** residents.

At least one WC for every **six** residents, separate from bath or shower room.

If any guest bedrooms have no washbasins, there should be a washbasin in the WC.

In the case of establishments with **four or less** bed spaces, it is acceptable for a bath or shower room to be combined with a washbasin and WC.

Additionally, where the maximum number of persons resident within an establishment, including proprietors is **no more than six**, it is acceptable that facilities are shared between guests and proprietors.

Where a shared arrangement exists, proprietors and their family should avoid prolonged use during the early to mid morning period, and the personal belongings of the proprietors and family should be removed from the rooms.

Hot water at all reasonable times.

N.B. Where establishments do not currently meet the above ratios but are willing and able to upgrade, they will be allowed until 1 July 2000 to do so.

Minimum Entry Requirements – En-suite Bathrooms (where provided)

The bath or shower and WC must be contained behind the main door of the bedroom.

Bedrooms with a washbasin, shower cabinet and en-suite WC are acceptable.

NB Freestanding in-bedroom showers do not count as en-suite facilities.

Fixtures and fittings

A bath or shower; if shower is provided it must have a shower screen or curtain.

Washbasin (minimum size suggested is 14" x 9.5" internal width) and mirror with light above or adjacent.

Soap dish.

A lidded WC.

Toilet roll holder.

A covered bin or open bin with sani bags.

A covered light.

Adequate ventilation in the form of an extractor fan or window that opens.

Windows require opaque curtain or blind.

Adequate heating (see below).*

A hook for clothes.

A non slip bath mat should be available on request where non slip baths are not provided.

A towel rail or equivalent (a radiator is not acceptable but a towel ring or a hanging rack on a radiator is).

Hot water for bathing should be available at all reasonable times.

Clean hand and bath towel per person.

Clean bath mat for each new let.

Fresh soap to be provided for each new guest.

Toilet tissue.

Electric razor point or adaptor to be available within easy reach of the mirror. This may be located in a bedroom or bathroom.

*Where there are no external walls/windows heat permeating from the bedroom may be adequate. En-suites with an external window will require heating. A heated towel rail is acceptable.

4 Bathrooms, shower rooms and en-suite facilities etc.

En-suite provision

Please note that while there is no specific minimum requirement for en-suite facilities, where they are provided, the ratios shown below will be taken into account in the assessment of the overall quality score.

Quality Score	1	2	3	4
Quality Indicators	Possibly no en-suite or private facilities.	At least 40% en-suite or private facilities.	At least 80% en-suite or private facilities.	

Minimum Entry Requirements – Private Bathrooms (where provided)

A private bathroom is one designated solely for the occupants of one bedroom.

The bathroom should be on the same floor reasonably close to the bedroom, lockable with a key provided.

Access to bath/shower rooms from bedroom through public areas, eg lounge, dining room etc is not acceptable.

Fixtures and fittings

The following should be provided – as for en-suites, but additionally:

A lock and key.

Bathrooms with an external window will require heating. A heated towel rail is acceptable.

Minimum Entry Requirements – Public Bathroom(s) (where provided)

Access to bath/shower rooms from a bedroom through public areas, eg lounge, dining room etc is not acceptable. No charge should be made for the use of these facilities.

Fixtures and fittings

The following should be provided, as for en-suites, but additionally:

All public bathrooms require heating.

Bath mat changed daily.

Soap need not be provided (already provided in bedrooms).

Internal lock or bolt.

4 Bathrooms, shower rooms and en-suite facilities etc.

Minimum Entry Requirements – Guest Toilets

Access to guest toilets from a bedroom through public areas, eg lounge, dining room etc is not acceptable.

Fixtures and fittings

A lidded WC.

A covered bin or open bin with sani bags.

Toilet roll holder.

A washbasin, where provided, to include hot water, soap and hand towel.

A covered light.

Adequate ventilation in the form of an extractor fan or window that opens.

Windows require an opaque curtain or blind.

An internal lock or bolt.

Toilet tissue.

Minimum Entry Requirements – Washbasins (where provided in the bedroom)

Fixtures and fittings

Minimum size suggested is 14" x 9.5" internal width. The acceptability will also depend on the shape, position of taps etc.

A towel rail or equivalent (a radiator is not acceptable but a towel ring or a hanging rack on a radiator is).

Hot water available.

Clean hand and bath towels per person.

Fresh soap to be provided for each new guest.

Electric razor point or adaptor to be available within easy reach of the mirror, may be located in a bedroom or bathroom.

4 Bathrooms, shower rooms and en-suite facilities etc.

Decoration

Quality Score	1	2	3	4
Quality Indicators	Functional decor with limited co-ordination.		Well maintained, practical decor; wall and ceiling covering well applied. All in good condition.	Excellent interior design.
				Professional finish to all aspects of decoration. Highest quality finish to wall coverings; well fitted, high quality tiles; grouting in excellent condition.
				Attractive use of decorative enhancements, where appropriate.

Fixtures and fittings

Quality Score	1	2	3	4	5
Quality Indicators	Fittings of an acceptable quality		Solid, matching, good quality and well fitted appliances. Co-ordinated sanitary ware.		Provision of bath and shower, with high quality fixtures and fittings, eg larger baths, shower cubicles or shower screens. Full size washbasin in bedroom or en-suite. Easy-to-use appliances.
	Correctly fitted flooring.		Well fitted, good quality flooring.		Professionally fitted, high quality flooring.
	Correctly fitted, appropriate window covering.		Well fitted window covering, with sufficient width and height to draw completely across the window.		High quality and well fitted window covering with ample drape and width.
	Adequate water pressure and satisfactory drainage.				Hot water to meet guest needs at all times.
	Flat surface available for guest belongings.		Good shelf space for guest belongings.		Ample and convenient shelf space for guest belongings.

Space and comfort

Quality Score	1	2	3	4	5
Quality Indicators	Adequate space with satisfactory layout and sufficient free movement.		Sufficient space to allow easy access to the facilities.		Ample space to allow easy access to the facilities.
	Convenient access to bath, shower and WC.				Convenient layout.
	Minimal noise from plumbing.				

4 Bathrooms, shower rooms and en-suite facilities etc.

Lighting and heating

Quality Score	1	2	3	4	5
Quality Indicators	Adequate lighting, appropriately positioned.		Well positioned lights giving good levels of illumination.		Well positioned good quality lights giving good levels of illumination for various purposes eg shaving, applying make-up etc.
			Good quality light fittings		
	Adequate heating for size of room.		Comfortable heating levels, appropriate to room size.		Responsive heating system, controlled by guest and available at all times.
	Effective ventilation.				Heated towel rail.

Towels and toiletries

Minimum Entry Requirements	Clean hand and bath towel per person, fresh soap to be provided for each new guest.				
Quality Score	1	2	3	4	5
Quality Indicators	Satisfactory quality, range and size of towels.		Matching range of good quality absorbent towels.		Provision of good range of quality towels, eg bathsheets, bathrobes and flannels.
	No evidence of proprietor's personal belongings.				
			Towels changed at least every 4 days, except where, as part of an environmental policy guests are invited and agree to a less frequent change of linen.		Towels changed daily, except where, as part of an environmental policy guests are invited and agree to a less frequent change of linen.
			Good quality toilet tissue and a range of quality toiletries.		Luxury toilet tissue and a good range of well presented quality toiletries, eg high quality soap, shampoo, shower gel, conditioner, tissues, cotton wool balls, cotton buds etc.

5 Guest meals – food quality

Breakfast

Minimum Entry Requirements	Full cooked breakfast to be available, if not it must be advertised as not being available and a substantial continental breakfast must be provided to include a selection of the following: cold meats, cheeses, fresh fruits, fruit compotes, preserves, cereals, juices, yoghurts, bakery items and hot beverages (choice of teas and coffees).

NB For cooked breakfast boiled eggs only are not acceptable.

Buffet style is acceptable.

Quality Score	1	2	3	4	5
Quality Indicators	Possibly a set menu with, for example, juice, cereal, bacon and egg, coffee and tea, toast. All hot foods should be well cooked and presented, with no excess grease on the plate, and served at the correct temperature.		A choice of good quality items available, eg fruit, choice of cereals, sausage, tomato, brown or white toast and a range of preserves. An attractive buffet (if provided).		High quality fresh ingredients and a wide choice of items, eg fresh fruit juices, fresh ground coffee, choice of teas, cheeses and cold meats, high quality bakery items and homemade preserves. Regional specialities and/or homemade items.
	Care should be taken to ensure that juices are chilled, toast is crisp and tea and coffee are freshly made.		Freshly cooked hot items served at the correct temperature, with eggs cooked to order.		Good use of fresh local/homegrown produce where available.

Dinner (where provided)

Quality Score	1	2	3	4	5
Quality Indicators	All food carefully prepared and presented and properly cooked. Food served at the correct temperature, on a hot or cold plate as appropriate.		Well presented food freshly cooked from good quality ingredients. Evidence of fresh foods being used.		Excellent home cooking with an emphasis on fresh, seasonal, local ingredients, skilfully cooked. Obvious care and attention to detail and thoughtful menu planning.
	Meals might be simply structured but freshly cooked on the premises.		Particular attention given to food quality rather than an extensive choice.		Strong emphasis on food quality.
	May be a set menu, but with an alternative available on request.				

6 Public areas

General

Minimum Entry Requirements

Corridors and stairs should be in good repair and free from obstruction.

A dining room/breakfast area available unless meals served only in the bedroom.

Adequate levels of lighting for safety and comfort in all public areas, including sufficient light on stairways and landings at night.

Provide an adequate level of heating in all public areas.

Tourist and travel information to be provided.

Breakfast/Dining room

Quality Score	1	2	3	4	5
Quality Indicators					An emphasis on quality throughout (see also Public Areas – decoration, below) with a harmonious combination of decor, lighting and heating.
					No intrusive noise or smells.
	Adequately sized tables and acceptable circulation space.		Good layout and adequate circulation space to allow staff and customers to pass without inconvenience.		High degree of comfort, well-spaced chairs, spacious tables.
	Convenient positioning of tables and chairs in sound, stable condition.		Appropriate table and chair heights.		Table and seating arrangements are such that there is evidence that guests' comfort has been fully considered.
	Table appointments of a satisfactory standard.		Well laid tables with matching cutlery and crockery. Flowers or other appropriate decoration on tables. Good quality paper napkins where appropriate.		Table appointment of the highest standard, quality accessories, good range of cutlery and glassware.
					High quality napery or well presented polished wood.
	Menus, where provided, possibly hand-written on a card, but clean and giving basic information.				Attractively presented menu and wine list, where provided, using clear, informative layout and helpful descriptions.

6 Public areas

Decoration

Quality Score	1	2	3	4	5
Quality Indicators	Functional decor and limited co-ordination.		Pleasing interior, with evidence of co-ordinated design. Well finished, good quality wall coverings and paintwork. Wall and ceiling coverings professionally applied. Use of pictures etc, where appropriate, particularly on plain walls.		Excellent interior design and overall impression. High quality wall coverings in excellent condition; professional finish to all aspects of decoration. Attractive use of pictures, prints and other decorative relief. Interesting architectural features, objects of interest, artwork, objets d'art, floral arrangements.

Furniture, furnishings and fittings

Quality Score	1	2	3	4	5
Quality Indicators	A sparing but adequate provision of furniture, furnishings and fittings, in terms of quality and quantity. Limited co-ordination.		Good quality furniture. Substantial, lined curtains. Good use of co-ordination. Well fitted, good quality flooring.		High quality modern, reproduction or antique furniture. High degree of comfort. Plush soft fabrics. Excellent co-ordination of furniture and fabrics. High quality carpet in excellent condition, professionally fitted, with good underlay. Well maintained polished floors with high quality rugs/mats where appropriate.

Space and comfort

Quality Score	1	2	3	4	5
Quality Indicators	Public areas possibly shared with proprietor, little evidence of personal belongings. Acceptable comfort and range of furniture. Adequate space for guest comfort. Acceptable environment for guests without disturbing levels of noise, music, smells, smoke, pets etc.		Public areas, including lounge where provided, designated for guest use. Range of sofas and/or armchairs. Sufficient space to allow a good degree of comfort for guests. Some personal touches, eg books, magazines, local historical information etc.		Comfortable lounge – generally separate from dining room. Good choice of comfortable seating. Ample space. Fresh and airy atmosphere.

6 Public areas

Lighting and heating

Quality Score	1	2	3	4	5
Quality Indicators	Adequate levels of lighting, appropriately positioned.		Good levels of controllable lighting in all areas.		Excellent lighting which creates a good effect and shows off rooms to their best advantage.
					Good levels of light for all practical purposes such as reading etc.
	Adequate levels of heating for guest comfort.		Particularly well lit stairs, landings and corridors.		
			Comfortable margin of heating to suit most guests.		A positive effort made to ensure that heating meets the guests' needs. Back up source of heat for very cold weather.
					Open fires where appropriate.
			Efficient heating according to season.		

General requirements

Safety and security

Minimum Entry Requirements

The entrance should be clearly identified with lighting above the doorway.

A high degree of general safety and security maintained, including information on procedures in the event of an emergency.

In addition there must be printed details of how to summon assistance in the event of an emergency at night.

Adequate measures provided for the security of guests and their property. There should be a means of securing bedroom doors from inside and out, and a key available. An exemption may be made in the case of architecturally listed or older properties where guests are advised in advance that bedroom doors can only be secured from the inside, and there is a facility within the establishment to secure guests valuables.

Provide adequate levels of lighting for safety and comfort in all public areas, including sufficient light on stairways and landings at night.

Car park, where provided, should also be adequately lit, to ensure guests' safety.

Particular attention should be given to the safety and security of guests occupying ground floor bedrooms.

7 General requirements

Maintenance and external appearance

Minimum Entry Requirements

Buildings, their fixtures, furnishings, fittings and exterior and interior decor must be maintained in a sound, clean condition and must be fit for the purpose intended.

All electrical equipment should be safely maintained and in good working order.

Quality Score	1	2	3	4	5
Quality Indicators – External	Exteriors of buildings maintained in a sound, clean condition. Adequately maintained property, overall. Neat appearance of outbuildings.	Well maintained property and outbuildings – some natural weathering may be present.		Excellent standards of external maintenance including outbuildings and signs, allowing for the age of the building. Fresh, well-maintained paintwork in a new building and in an older building, no unsightly staining to stonework	
	Overall tidiness, including window boxes, hanging baskets, tubs etc, where appropriate.	Attractive use of window boxes, hanging baskets and tubs where appropriate. Where displayed, signs to be maintained in good condition.		Attractive architectural features and decorations.	

Quality Score	1	2	3	4	5
Quality Indicators – Internal	Equipment working as intended. All decor, furniture and fittings in satisfactory condition.	All equipment in good working order and well maintained.		High standard of maintenance.	
	Some signs of normal wear and tear. Well secured fittings, eg door knobs, lamp shades etc.	Few signs of wear and tear visible to decor, furniture and fittings. Signs of attention to detail.		No significant evidence of wear and tear to decor, furniture and fittings. Care and attention to detail is obvious.	

Parking (where provided)

Quality Score	1	2	3	4	5
Quality Indicators	Reasonably easy, safe and adequately maintained parking.		Easy access. Well maintained surface.		Ample car parking spaces.
	Limited attempt to control parking.		Clear definition of parking area. Adequate lighting.		Good, well positioned lighting. Consideration given to the security of guests' cars.

7 General requirements

Grounds and gardens (where provided)

Quality Score	1	2	3	4	5
Quality Indicators	An adequate first impression (eg washing line discreetly positioned). Safe pathways. No litter.		Well maintained and tidy.		Attractively maintained – well tended borders or shrubs, tidy pathways and edges, lawns in good condition and well cut, hedges trimmed and an overall attempt to maintain an attractive appearance throughout the year.
	Adequately maintained driveway or access.		Well maintained driveways, footpaths etc. Attractive overall appearance.		Good attention to detail, including landscaping, driveways, the provision of garden furniture or architectural features (eg gazebo, pergola, summer house etc).

Environment

Quality Score	1	2	3	4	5
Quality Indicators	Satisfactory first impression. Acceptable noise levels.		Even in heavily urbanised areas, evidence that real effort has been made to compensate for poor surroundings.		Establishment is inviting. Provides an air of well being. Attractive surroundings, convenient location, or a secluded situation in extensive grounds with splendid views etc are examples of factors that will be considered in assessment.

Annexes

Minimum Entry Requirements

Where an establishment has an annexe, the facilities provided in the annexe will be taken into account in determining the overall suitability of the establishment. Paths or passageways to the annexe must be in good condition, well surfaced and adequately lit.

Visitors must be advised at the time of booking and subsequently of any change, if the accommodation offered is in an unconnected annexe, or has separate external access; guests should be informed of the location of such accommodation.

7 General requirements

Extra facilities

These are facilities and services which may be provided within the establishment. They are optional requirements, but if provided the quality, range, presentation, ease of use will be taken into account in the assessment of the quality score. Examples might include: swimming pool, nature trail, indoor and outdoor sports and games, farm visits, craft shop, additional food and beverage facilities, TV lounge and room service.

Quality Score	1	2	3	4	5
Quality Indicators	Very limited range of additional features, if any.		Good range of additional features	Excellent range of additional features	

Statutory obligations

Minimum Entry Requirements	Fulfilment of the statutory obligations, where applicable, including:
	Fire Precautions
	Price Display Orders
	Food Safety
	Licensing
	Health and Safety
	Disability Discrimination
	Trade Descriptions
	Proprietors may be asked to provide evidence that **Public Liability Cover is being maintained** and that the above requirements are being fulfilled.

NATIONAL
ACCESSIBLE
SCHEME

FOR SERVICED &
SELF-CATERING
ACCOMMODATION

FOR WHEELCHAIR USERS AND
OTHERS
WITH MOBILITY PROBLEMS

English
Tourist Board

CRITERIA

The national tourist boards for England, Scotland and Wales operate a national ACCESSIBLE scheme to identify and acknowledge those places to stay that meet the needs of wheelchair users and others with limited mobility. There are three Categories of accessibility:

Category 1 Accessible to a wheelchair user travelling independently

Category 2 Accessible to a wheelchair user travelling with assistance

Category 3 Accessible to someone with limited mobility, able to walk a few paces and up a maximum of three steps

The minimum requirements for each of the three Categories are shown in this leaflet. It is emphasised that these are minimum requirements. If an Access inspection reveals that there are other aspects, not dealt with in the criteria, that prohibit access or present serious obstacles, the awarding of an Accessible Category may be withheld until such time as it is confirmed that the situation has been remedied.

PLEASE NOTE:

The measurements included in these criteria are those acceptable to meet the requirements of the three Categories of accessibility. They are not, necessarily, recommended or ideal measurements. Details of recommended measurements are given in the 'Providing Accessible Accommodation' guide published by the English Tourist Board and Holiday Care Service. Copies, price £5, can be obtained from Holiday Care Service, 2nd Floor, Imperial Building, Victoria Road, Horley, Surrey RH6 7PZ or from your regional tourist board.

NOTES:

1. Ramps, where present, should not have a gradient at any point of more than 1:12. Removable ramps, unless permanently in situ, are not acceptable for Category 1.

2. Single steps: For Category 2 there can be a succession of single steps, provided there is sufficient space after each step for a wheelchair to sit comfortably and safely, with all four wheels on the ground.

3. Steps to be used by a disabled guest should have risers no more than 19cm, treads no less than 25cm deep and 75cm wide.

4. For Category 1, thresholds to rooms to which the wheelchair user requires access must be no higher than 2cm.

PUBLIC ENTRANCE		
CATEGORY 3	CATEGORY 2	CATEGORY 1
A public entrance must be accessible to wheelchair users from a setting down or car parking point		
Where an establishment has a car park, a reservable parking space should be available for a disabled guest, on request		If there is a car park there must be a level reservable space with a minimum width of 3.6 metres for each bedroom meeting the Category 1 requirements
The route from the parking point or space to the entrance must be sound and free from obstacles. Deep gravel, cobbles and pot-holed surfaces are unlikely to be acceptable		The route from parking point or space to the entrance must be level or ramped
The entrance door must have a clear opening of not less than 70cm		
Where there is no ramp there must be no more than 3 steps, at any one point, to the entrance	Where threre is no ramp there must be no more than single steps to the entrance (See Notes 2 and 3 on Criteria page)	The threshold at the entrance must be no higher than 2cm
Within the reception area there must be an unobstructed space of not less than 110x70cm		

INTERIOR GENERAL		
CATEGORY 3	CATEGORY 2	CATEGORY 1
Those public passageways that lead to the restaurant or dining room, lounge, TV lounge (unless TV is provided in the bedroom), bar, the disabled guest's bedroom and bathroom (if other than ensuite) should be not less than 75cm wide	Those public passageways that lead to the restaurant or dining room, lounge, TV lounge (unless TV is provided in the bedroom), bar, the disabled guest's bedroom and bathroom (if other than ensuite) should be not less than 80cm wide and not less than 120cm opposite the doors to the rooms the disabled guest will be required to use	
Doors to the rooms referred to above should have a clear opening of not less than 70cm	Doors to the rooms referred to above should have a clear opening of not less than 75cm	
There must be no more than 3 steps, at any one point, in the corridors the disabled guest will be required to use or at the entrance of the rooms referred to above	There must be no more than single steps, at any one point, in the corridors or to the rooms the disabled guest will be required to use	All routes to be used by the disabled guest must be level or ramped
		Access to the restaurant/ dining room, lounge, bar, bedroom, bathroom and WC (where not ensuite) must be level or ramped with thresholds no higher than 2 cm
	In the restaurant/dining room there must be at least one accessible table with a clear underspace of at least 65cm high. Blocks, to lift a table when required, are acceptable. Where three or more bedrooms meet the requirements for Category 2 or 1, at least two such accessible tables should be provided	
Where the disabled guest may be required to use a lift, the door should have a clear opening of not less than 70cm, and the interior of the lift should be not less than 110cm deep by 70cm wide	Where the disabled guest may be required to use a lift, the door should have a clear opening of not less than 75cm, and the interior of the lift should be not less than 120cm deep by 80cm wide	
		Where the guest is required to use a lift it must have automatic doors and the controls must be 140cm or less above the floor

BEDROOM (only one bedroom need meet these requirements)		
CATEGORY 3	CATEGORY 2	CATEGORY 1
	There must be unobstructed space of not less than 110 x 70cm	
	There must be space alongside at least one side of the bed of not less than 80cm to allow for lateral transfer	
		The surface of the bed must be between 45-54cm above the floor
		Door handles, light switches, TV controls, curtain pulls, wardrobe rails, etc, should be accessible and not more than 140cm above the floor
		Light switch and telephone (where provided) no more than 50cm from the bed

BATHROOM		
	Categories 1 and 2: Only one bathroom, separate or ensuite with the bedroom(s) above need meet these requirements	
CATEGORY 3	**CATEGORY 2**	**CATEGORY 1**
The bathroom must be ensuite or on the same floor as the disabled guest's bedroom		
		The door handle and light switch must be 140cm or less above the floor
	There must be an unobstructed interior space, clear of the door swing, of not less than 100 x 70cm	
Where a bath is provided it should have a horizontal or angled support rail on the far side (recommended) 25cm above the rim)		The horizontal or angled support rail at the far side of the bath must be no more than 30cm above the rim
	Where a bath is provided there must be space alongside of not less than 80cm to allow for lateral transfer	
		The rim of the bath must be 45-50cm above the floor
Where a shower only is provided, it must have a seat (recommended 45-50cm above the floor) and a support rail on the far wall (recommended 25cm above top of the seat and a maximum of 50cm from the centre of the seat)		
	Where a shower only is provided it must have a level entry i.e. no rim, a lateral transfer space of not less than 80cm, a seat	
		Where a shower only is available to the guest the controls must be 140cm or less above the floor
Where there is a step into the shower, it should have a riser of no more than 19cm		
There must be a washbasin within the bathroom or bedroom	The washbasin, either within the bathroom or bedroom, must have sufficient clear underspace and/or lever taps to enable it to be used by someone in a wheelchair	

WC		
	Categories 1 and 2: Only one WC, separate or ensuite with the bedroom(s) above need meet these requirements	
CATEGORY 3	CATEGORY 2	CATEGORY 1
The WC must be ensuite or on the same floor as the disabled guest's bedroom		
Toilet paper must be within reach of the seat		
	There must be a lateral transfer space to the WC of not less than 80cm	
	The rim of the WC seat must be between 45-50cm above the floor	
	There must be a horizontal or angled support rail opposite the transfer space, between 20-30cm above the seat	
		The horizontal or angled support rail opposite the transfer space must be no more than 50cm from the centre of the seat
Where the WC is separate from the bathroom there must be a washbasin in the same room	If separate from the bathroom there must be an unobstructed interior space of not less than 110 x 70cm and a washbasin with clear underspace	

WELCOME ALL

The practical answer to better service for customers with disabilities and special needs

Welcome All is a one-day course, developed by the English Tourist Board in association with the Holiday Care Service. It provides an effective introduction to the expectations of special needs customers through the use of video, participative exercises and personal action plans. The focus is on awareness and personal understanding, and on techniques and actions to improve the quality of service you provide.

Taking part in the course will give you a practical perspective on the requirements of those with a range of disabilities and special service needs. It will help you to make your communication more effective and achieve a widespread improvement in customer service. The programme is offered at low cost. To find out more, please contact your Regional Tourist Board.

Glossary

A la carte. A menu offering multiple choice. 'From the bill of fare.'

Annual accounts. A summary of business financial transactions over the year and usually prepared by an accountant for submission to the Inland Revenue. In the case of a company, the accounts must be filed at Companies House.

Annual Percentage Rate (APR). The true rate of interest charged on a loan calculated over the year.

Bain marie. A piece of kitchen equipment for keeping liquids or vegetables hot. Can be dry or a receptacle full of water.

Balance sheet. A statement of the assets and liabilities of a business at a particular point in time.

Break-even figure. The amount a business needs to take to pay its way, *ie* to make neither a profit nor a loss.

Bullet points. Information listed in a short, punchy style.

Business plan. A document which is prepared for a lender in support of an application for funds, setting out the business activities and objectives in detail with worked forecasts.

Business rate. A tax on businesses calculated by multiplying the rateable value by the uniform poundage (fixed nationally).

Business transfer agent. One who specialises in the sale or transfer of businesses and business premises.

Carte du jour. Menu of the day.

Cashflow forecast. A detailed estimate of the money coming into and going out from a business over a period of time.

Contract of employment. A legally-binding contract between an employer and an employee. Can be written or unwritten.

Copy. Matter ready for printing.

Creditor. A firm or individual to whom money is owed.

Crown Court. A court superior to a Magistrates' Court and presided over by a Judge.

Debtor. A firm or individual owing money.

Demi-pension. See half board.

Depreciation. A measurement of the reduction in value of an asset over a period of time.

Fixed assets. Property or assets in a balance sheet such as buildings, fixtures and fittings not intended for sale but for use within the business.

Fixed costs. See overheads.

Fixtures and fittings. All equipment included in the sale of a business and not forming part of the actual building.

Full board. Bed and all meals.

Goodwill. An amount included in the value of the business over and above the net assets and reflecting its profitability.

Gross profit. Income less direct costs expressed as a percentage.

Half board. Bed, breakfast and one of the main meals.

Intoxicating liquor. Liquid with an original gravity not less than 1016 (1.2 per cent alcohol). Does not include flavouring essences, perfumes and medicines.

Job description. (Or job specification.) A written summary of the title, purpose, tasks, duties, *etc* of a job made out prior to filling a vacancy.

Lease. A contract, letting or renting of a property for a term. The owner is the lessor, the person or firm to whom a property is leased is the tenant or lessee.

Leasehold property. Property held by a tenant under a lease.

Liabilities. Amounts owed by a business to others.

Licensing Justices. A committee of magistrates who determine applications for licences to sell intoxicating liquor.

Media. Plural of medium, usually meaning the press, radio, television and other means of disseminating information.

Media pack. A pack sent to potential advertisers by a publisher and usually consisting of a rate card, a sample of the publication and a readership profile.

Net profit. Income less total costs.

Overdraft. The amount a bank is prepared to extend as credit on a current account.

Overheads. The day-to-day running costs of a business over and above the direct costs (supplies of food and drink).

Partnership. An agreement between two or more persons to trade as one entity.

Pay As You Earn (PAYE). A scheme under which employers have to collect income tax from their employees on behalf of the Government.

Pension. A scheme, usually operated by an insurance company, to provide an income on retirement.

Planning permission. Legal permission granted by a Local Authority to erect a new structure (including signs), to extend an existing one or to change the use of a property.

Profit and loss account. (Or Trading and Profit and Loss Account.) A statement showing income, expenditure and profit (or loss) for an accounting period, usually one year.

Rate card. A list of advertising rates.

Readership profile. An analysis of those who read a publication.

Registered office. The address at which a company is officially registered with the Registrar of Companies. (Seldom its trading address.)

Residential licence. A licence allowing the holder to sell intoxicating liquor to residents and bona fide guests.

Restaurant licence. A licence allowing the holder to sell intoxicating liquor as an ancillary to table meals.

Single column centimetre (scc). The usual unit of measuring advertising space, viz one column wide and one centimetre deep.

Sole proprietor (or trader). A self-employed person who owns and usually runs a business without a partner and not forming a limited company.

Split the. The way in which a purchase/selling price is divided into 'property', 'fixtures and fittings' and 'goodwill'.

Table d'hôte. Meal at a fixed price either without choice or with a limited choice of main course. (Literally 'host's table'.)

Tax relief. That which is obtained by legally setting expenditure against profits.

Turnover. What comes into the business from all sources.

Uniform rate (or poundage). The multiplier set annually on a national basis for business rates.

VAT (value added tax). A tax administered by HM Customs and Excise and applied to goods and services when turnover is above a certain threshold. (Usually fixed annually in the Budget.)

Index

COPING WITH SELF ASSESSMENT
How to complete your tax return and minimise your tax bill

John Whitley

'If you dare to do your own tax return, this book needs to be on your bookshelf.' Laurel Alexander, *Working From Home.* Save time and money with this step-by-step-guide. It takes you through everything from completing the forms correctly to surviving an Inland Revenue enquiry. What do you do if you make an error in your claim and how do you make payments on account? The answers are all here, together with ways to avoid penalties, interest and surcharges, plus a chapter on paying less tax. John Whiteley is a Chartered Accountant who has successfully advised taxpayers from all walks of life.

160pp. illus. 1 85703 580 1. 4th edition

MAKING DIRECT MAIL WORK
Get great results from all your direct mail

Peter Arnold

Direct Mail is a proven and effective method of promotion for almost every type of organisation, large or small. Love it or hate it, direct mail works. Any small company, or even self-employed people, can take advantage of this most flexible and controllable of all promotional media. This book sets out, in a simple and graphic way, exactly how to initiate and run your own direct mail system. It also shows you how to avoid the pitfalls and maximise effectiveness and efficiency. Peter Arnold has been creating and writing direct mail campaigns for over 35 years, and is one of the most experienced professionals in Britain. He has worked for every sort of organisation from the large multinational to the one and two-man operation.

120pp. illus. 1 85703 297 7.

MANAGING YOUR BUSINESS ACCOUNTS
How to keep the books and maintain financial control over your business

Peter Taylor

Now in its fifth edition and updated to take account of recent changes in the law, students as well as business managers will find this book refreshingly simple and easy to use. 'It will help you to sort out the best way to carry out double entry book-keeping, as well as providing a clear step-by-step guide to accounting procedures.' *Mind Your Own Business*. 'Takes one through the basic steps in simple language.' *Western Morning News*. 'Compulsory reading both for those starting a new business, and those already in the early stages.' *Manager, National Westminster Bank (Midlands)*. Peter Taylor is a Fellow of the Institute of Chartered Accountants. He has many years' practical experience of advising small businesses, especially on taxation and auditing matters.

184pp. illus. 1 85703 536 4. 5th edition.

MASTERING BOOK-KEEPING
A complete step-by-step guide to the principles of accounting

Peter Marshall

Illustrated at every stage with specimen entries, the book will be an ideal companion for students taking LCCI, RSA, BTEC, accountancy technician and similar courses at schools, colleges or training centres. Typical business transactions are used to illustrate all the essential theory, practice and skills required to be effective in a real business setting. 'An interesting approach.' *Association of Business Executives Journal*. 'A complete step-by-step guide . . . each section of the book teaches a useful skill in its own right.' *OwnBase*. 'In addition to providing a useful approach to the teaching and learning of book-keeping skills, the way in which the text is presented should ensure that the book also provides a valuable reference source for revision and prompting.' *Teeline*.

192pp. illus. 1 85703 495 3. 4th edition.

STARTING YOUR OWN BUSINESS
How to plan and build a successful enterprise

Jim Green

Now in its second edition, this dynamic guide explores the vital steps to creating a business. It shows you how to conceptualise, set up and operate any small business successfully, from preparing a business plan and launching the venture, to developing marketing strategies and selling techniques. 'Practical advice presented in a clear and concise style.'*Moneywise*. 'An easy-to read and motivating book.' *Making Money*. Jim Green writes and lectures on business topics.

160pp. illus. 1 85703 274 8. 2nd edition

DELIVERING CUSTOMER SERVICE
How to win a competitive edge through managing customer relationships successfully

Sheila Payne

'. . .gives guidance on developing positive working relationships and how to solve problems and initiate and evaluate changes on customers' behalf.' *Customer Service Management*. A practical, no-nonsense guide for everyone who deals with customers. The book covers the criteria for NVQ Levels 2 and 3 in Customer Service.

184pp. illus. 1 85703 486 4. 2nd edition.